10 Strategies for Reentering the Workforce

10 Strategies for Reentering the Workforce

Career Advice for Anyone Who Needs a Good (or Better) Job *Now*

Mary E. Ghilani

Westport, Connecticut
London

Library of Congress Cataloging-in-Publication Data

Ghilani, Mary E., 1958–

10 strategies for reentering the workforce : career advice for anyone who needs a good (or better) job now / Mary E. Ghilani.

p. cm.

Includes bibliographical references and index.

ISBN 978-0-313-35696-4 (alk. paper)

1. Vocational guidance—United States. 2. Career changes—United States. 3. Job hunting—United States. I. Title. II. Title: Ten strategies for reentering the workforce.

HF5382.5.U5G46 2009

650.14—dc22   2008037821

British Library Cataloguing in Publication Data is available.

Library of Congress Catalog Card Number: 2008037821

ISBN: 978-0-313-35696-4

First published in 2009

Praeger Publishers, 88 Post Road West, Westport, CT 06881

An imprint of Greenwood Publishing Group, Inc.

www.praeger.com

Printed in the United States of America

The paper used in this book complies with the Permanent Paper Standard issued by the National Information Standards Organization (Z39.48–1984).

10 9 8 7 6 5 4 3 2 1

Contents

Acknowledgments

I would like to thank all of the people who helped me at significant points along my career. Special thanks to my husband, Chuck, for his suggestions and encouragement; to my former professors Lori Bruch and LeeAnn Eschbach, for their knowledge and support; and to the students who visited the Career Services office at Luzerne County Community College over the years. Last, but not least, thanks and appreciation to my editor, Jeff Olson, and the staff at Praeger Publishing.

Introduction

As the director of a career center at a community college, I see a number of job seekers requesting help to find a new job or career. Many of these individuals have suddenly found themselves unemployed because of a company closing or corporate downsizing, are newly divorced or widowed or are single parents, or simply want to find a better job. During the course of our conversation, I too often hear people lament, "I wish I'd done this sooner," or, "I wish I could be a (fill in the blank)," or, "I should have done *that* job." These statements are usually followed up with, "But *now* it's too late" or, "I'm too old" or, "It (school) will take too long, or cost too much."

This book was written to help you see that it is possible to find a better job or improve your employment situation no matter your age or what stage you are in your career. Given the changes in today's world of work, and after listening to my students and clients over the years, I have developed a new philosophy regarding work: Doing a job that you enjoy, even if it means going back to school to obtain it, is better than staying in a low-paying or unhappy employment situation for the rest of your career.

If you are reading this book because you were recently laid off, are considering returning to the workforce after an absence, or just need to find a better job, welcome! I have developed ten basic strategies to help you find a better job. The chapters do not necessarily need to be read in order, but you will gain the best use of the book if you start from the beginning and progress until the end.

The first chapter provides an overview of the changing world in which we work. This chapter is especially useful if you have been out of the workforce for some time or have been at one job for a number of years. Chapters 2 through 4 will ask you to assess your present situation, set priorities, and identify your work-related strengths and skills and will discuss common emotions associated with job change or job loss. Chapter 5 will walk you through the career decision-making process if you are uncertain about what career or line of work to pursue next. Chapters 6 and 7 will explore your employment options, help you overcome the "yes, buts" and other common obstacles that prevent most people from enjoying a more satisfying work life, and discuss the process of creating an action plan to implement your career goals. Chapter 8 will ask you to choose a career direction and then create a plan of action to either go back to school or reenter the job market. Chapters 9 and 10 contain helpful tips and resources for finding a new job or going back to school.

Because not all job changers share the same experiences or have the same set of circumstances or priorities, practical suggestions are provided for each particular type of job seeker. Even in today's turbulent economic times, there are more options available than ever before to obtain the type of work life you desire. Regardless of your personal circumstances or how many years you have been in the workforce, most of us have more choices about our jobs than we realize.

Chapter 1

Understand Today's Workplace

People who work sitting down get paid more than people who work standing up.
Ogden Nash

Most of us were raised with the idea of going to school, finding a good job, and staying with that job until we retired. Those were the life lessons of success we learned from our parents, our neighbors, and our teachers. Unfortunately, we're not in our parents' workplace anymore. It will be unlikely for people entering the workforce today to have a job for life. They will hold a number of jobs in different industries, will have to be more flexible in the way they actually carry out their work, and must be prepared to pay for some of their own health and retirement benefits. The majority of workers will be employed by small firms, and more work will be contracted, outsourced, and performed part time. E-commerce will continue to impact the American workplace and will give more people with disabilities a chance to find jobs that use computer technologies. Even what we wear to work has changed as many companies adopt a more casual style of dress instead of the traditional shirt and tie.

For individuals reentering the workforce after a period of time, it may feel like they are entering an alien world. Procedures have changed, new technology has replaced standard office equipment, and there are new rules and regulations that must be followed. For those of you who have recently found yourselves thrust into the job market because of downsizing or layoffs, the very process of trying to find work in today's job market may seem foreign and overwhelming. If you have decided to make a major career change, such as moving from a manufacturing environment to an office setting, adjusting to a new workplace setting can be a major culture shock.

MOOD AND TONE

You can't turn on the television or pick up a newspaper without seeing a story about a company closing or someone being laid off. In addition to all of the normal workplace stresses, employees are worried about whether or not they will have a job—and for how long. Most of us personally know people who have been downsized, right-sized, or laid off during the middle of their careers. Values such as job loyalty and perceptions of what we owe a company and what they owe us have been shattered as more and more companies close their offices and move overseas to gain a more competitive edge. The ability to provide for our families after retirement is a new concern that wasn't there ten years ago because many companies have discontinued offering pensions or health care benefits after retirement. Stock market fluctuations and well-publicized events such as the Enron scandal and other financial mismanagement by corporate executives have created a higher than normal level of tension, uncertainty, anger, and other forms of job stress for employees today.

SECURITY ISSUES

Since the events of 9/11, homeland and workplace security have become another part of our daily routine. It is not uncommon to hear stories of shootings in restaurants, churches, schools, and in other public places that we used to assume were safe. Security breaches at high-level research facilities, Internet leaks, and information theft all require individuals and businesses to tighten their security measures. The development of new degree programs in cyber security illustrates the changes in the way that companies now conduct business. All of these factors impact the way we work and result in minor inconveniences that affect everything from where we park our car to how we open our office and log onto our computer.

WORK VALUES

The concept of company loyalty is a faded relic of our parents' generation. Watching neighbors, coworkers, and even our parents lose their jobs after years of service has changed our perspective on company loyalty. In today's world of work, the employer does not have to keep us employed forever. The new twenty-first century employment contract involves a series of temporary assignments. This behooves us to keep our skills updated, our resumes current, and to take advantage of any training or continuing education opportunities that may arise.

All of these changes have resulted in a level of job mobility that was not imaginable in our parents' day. Today, it is acceptable to move from job to job to advance yourself. For many people, jobs are also not an all-consuming passion or the total makeup of their identity, as they were in the 1980s. More time for family and value-added work has replaced sacrifice and loyalty to the company. Unlike their predecessors, today's workers do not feel the need to make excuses to leave the office early to attend a child's soccer game or band concert.

TECHNOLOGY ADVANCES

Being computer literate is now an absolute requirement in almost any job. Everyone must know how to search for information on the Internet, schedule appointments via an electronic calendar system, and communicate by e-mail. In medical offices, for example, computerized scheduling and billing software have replaced appointment books and paper insurance forms. Executives who aren't able to use computers to do research or use Microsoft Word or an Excel spreadsheet are considered out of touch. Rather than playing telephone tag, instant messaging and e-mail have become faster and easier methods of communicating. The use of electronic meeting software and video conferencing has allowed us to transcend geographic boundaries. We are living in a time in which technology changes at light speed. With every new product or upgrade, technology will continue to impact our offices and improve the way we do business. Unfortunately, employees who cannot adapt to the new technology will have limited options in today's workforce.

DEMOGRAPHICS

The makeup of workers has changed as well. Today, the workplace is made up of people from all ages and backgrounds. In some companies, it is as common to work with someone who grew up in your hometown as it is to work with someone from India or Russia. The rich diversity of workers not only includes individuals of varying race, gender, ethnicity, and religious background but also those who differ in physical ability, parental status, age, sexual orientation, ideology, socioeconomic status, or geographic background.

There are more women in the workforce today than ever before. More women are not only working full time, they are working all year long rather than just during the months when their children are in school. In addition, many businesses are now owned by women. Women-owned firms represent 30% of all U.S. businesses, and women entrepreneurs are among the fastest growing groups of business owners.[1]

According to the U.S. Census Bureau, immigration accounted for only about 21% of our nation's population growth in the 1900s. However, between 2000 and 2016, the Bureau expects that international migration will account for more than half of our nation's population growth, with the fastest growth in the number of Hispanic and Asian immigrants.[2]

Marketplace globalization, outsourcing, and relaxed trade restrictions have resulted in American companies being owned by, or doing business with, countries in every corner of the world. It is not uncommon for people to conduct business with clients from other countries or for office personnel and administrators to talk with staff at a sister plant in London or Germany. Being able to get along and communicate effectively with workers from different backgrounds and all walks of life has become crucial in today's business world.

The other major change is the increase in the number of older workers in the workplace. Over the past few decades, the U.S. economy has benefited from a labor force that has grown faster than the overall population. However, starting in 2010, a demographic shift will begin, resulting in a large increase in the sixty-five and over age group and a decline of the twenty to sixty-four age group,[3] which will result in a decrease in the available labor pool. By 2030, the U.S. Census predicts over seventy-one million Americans will be sixty-five years or older.[4] A 2004 survey by the American Association for Retired Persons (AARP) found that 79% of boomers plan to work in some capacity during their retirement years.[5] With more and more boomers delaying retirement for economic and social reasons, we will see a much larger population of older workers in the workforce. Both younger and older workers alike will have to learn how to deal with and respect the intergenerational differences arising from their respective ages, life experiences, work values, and familiarity with technology.

WORK SCHEDULES

Many companies are now open for longer hours and more days in the week than was the case twenty years ago. It is not uncommon, for example, for large supermarkets to be open twenty-four hours a day. Companies that work with parent or sister firms in other countries may need to conduct their business over different time zones. The advance of communication technology has allowed companies to operate outside of a traditional nine to five, Monday to Friday work schedule and offer flexible work schedules to their employees. Depending on the type of business and the needs of its clientele or production patterns, employees may work a flexible eight-hour day, a flexible-variable hour day that allows employees to vary the length of the work day as well as the arrival and departure times, or a compressed schedule consisting of four ten-hour days or cycles of twelve-hour shifts on the job and twelve-hour shifts off the job.

OFFICE ENVIRONMENT

The traditional office consists of a desk, chair, lamp, bookshelf, and a secretary seated out front. With the advent of laptop computers, the Internet, and sophisticated wireless and digital telecommunication systems, today's employees can work from their kitchen table, on the golf course, or in their car. Many workers report for duty at smaller offices or manufacturing plants connected by information networks and sophisticated shipping infrastructure. With a wireless laptop and a cell phone, many business executives and sales reps only need find a wireless hotspot to be able to conduct their business. Other forms of flexible work environments include *teleworking* or *telecommuting* (involves working at home or at a location other than the main office by using a computer or other telecommunications technology) and *hot desking* (a situation in which a physical space, containing a desk and PC, is available to anyone working on a flexible schedule).[6]

EDUCATIONAL LEVEL

Today, a college education is needed to be competitive in the job market. A 2007 report published in *Education Week* looked at the skills required to get jobs in every state and concluded that, at both the state and national level, people need to complete at least some college to earn a decent wage.[7] As advances in technology continue, higher levels of education are needed even for blue-collar jobs like welding, manufacturing, and auto repair.

In general, occupations that require more formal education or training have higher pay and benefits.[8] According to the 2006 to 2016 employment projections from the Bureau of Labor Statistics, the typical qualification for half of the thirty fastest-growing occupations is a bachelor's degree or higher.[9] These jobs include physical therapists, physician assistants, financial advisors, computer systems analysts, database and network systems administrators, software engineers, substance abuse and mental health counselors, forensic science technicians, health and medical technicians, data communications and network analysts, veterinarians, and dental hygienists. Four of the thirty fastest-growing occupations require an associate degree. These include veterinary technicians, physical therapist assistants, dental hygienists, and environmental science and protection technicians. The remaining fastest-growing occupations require some form of job training. These include dental assistants, manicurists, personal and home care aides, and medical assistants.

EMPLOYEE SKILLS AND CHARACTERISTICS

For most of the twentieth century, our economy was based on agriculture and manufacturing. As technology improved, low-skilled jobs were replaced by automation, and the jobs that did remain required a higher level of sophistication and skills to manage the technology. More recently, globalization has dramatically altered our market by moving the remaining unskilled jobs overseas. As our country moved to a service- and knowledge-based economy, jobs required a more diverse set of skills that favor workers with a higher education. To demonstrate how skill levels have changed over the past fifty years, data from the Bureau of Labor Statistics show that, in 1950, unskilled workers made up 60% of the workforce and skilled and professional workers made up 20% of the workforce. By 1991, professionals still comprised 20% of the job market, but less than 35% were unskilled and more than 45% were skilled workers. In 2005, skilled workers made up 65% of the workforce, professionals made up 24%, and unskilled workers only made up 15% of the workforce.[10] The unskilled labor market represents jobs that require a high school diploma or less. What these changes tell us is that today's employees must have some type of skills training or education beyond high school to find work in our competitive job market.

Today's workers are faced with an environment in which career upheavals occur without warning. Corporate restructuring, downsizing, mergers, and decisions to increase profits affect workers whose jobs were thought to be secure for life. Even educational institutions, government agencies, and health care institutions have been faced with making difficult decisions that result in the reduction of their workforce. Unemployment can affect professionals at all levels as well as blue collar workers.

Adaptability is a trait that is fast becoming essential for survival and success in the American workplace. According to the theories of work adjustment, researchers describe the traits of adaptive performance as 1) ability to solve novel or complex problems by generating new ideas or new approaches to solving problems, 2) ability to deal with emergencies and crises by reacting appropriately and remaining clear-headed and focused, 3) demonstration of a willingness to learn new approaches and technology, 4) demonstration of interpersonal adaptability by listening to other's views, being open-minded and flexible, and tailoring one's own behavior to influence and work effectively with others, 5) ability to adjust appropriately to others' cultural differences and customs, 6) ability to cope with work stress by remaining calm in difficult circumstances and demonstrating resiliency, 7) ability to adjust to the physical changes in the work environment, and 8) ability to cope with uncertainty and ambiguity.[11]

Loyalty and hard work are no longer enough to compete in today's job market. Along with increased educational requirements, new skill requirements have also emerged. Today, employers want employees who are able to think and problem solve, who are technologically savvy and flexible, who work well in teams, possess good communication skills, and are willing to update their professional skills and abilities to meet the changing needs of whatever company or organization they work for. Employees who are not able, or not willing, to learn new procedures or use new technology will be quickly replaced with younger, less-expensive hires. As advances in technology and globalization continue, the demand for college-educated workers is expected to persist, as is the need for these employees to possess skills in reasoning, problem-solving, and interpersonal skills.[12]

Companies began downsizing and re-engineering their operations in the 1990s to survive in the marketplace. Since then, there has been a trend toward generalization rather than specialization. From a business owner's perspective, it is simply cheaper and more efficient for companies to hire one person to do several related tasks than it is to hire two separate individuals or pay a huge salary to someone whose services could be hired on a consultant basis as needed. As a result of downsizing, today's workers have become cross-trained generalists rather than specialists in their particular field. We can see examples of this in our school systems, where math teachers are being asked to teach computer science classes and coaches to double as health teachers or guidance counselors. The good news is that this trend provides more opportunities for people who want to work on a freelance, part-time, or consultant basis. Today, those who have acquired a particular expertise in one or two areas of their field (i.e., have become specialists) can usually find work running their own consulting firms or offering their services on a freelance basis.

FUTURE CAREER TRENDS

Health care, education, science and engineering, and sales and customer service are a few of the careers that continue to offer the promise of employment in the future. According to Elaine Chao, secretary of the Department of Labor, our country will need 900,000 engineers and 3.5 million new teachers, trainers, and researchers by 2014.[13] As America's population matures, the health care industry will need 3.4 million more health care professionals and more than 1.2 million registered nurses.[14]

According to the 2006 to 2016 projections from the U.S. Bureau of Labor Statistics, health care occupations are projected to gain the most new jobs followed by education, training, and library occupations.[15] Within the professional occupations group, three specific occupations expected to gain the most new jobs, more than half a million each, are registered nurses, retail salespersons, and customer service representatives.[16] Of those three occupations, registered nurses will earn the highest wages.

The fastest-growing occupation is expected to be network systems and data communication analysts followed by personal and home care aides, home health aides, and computer software engineers. Computer applications software engineers earned the highest wages in 2006. Although information systems are at the top of this list, eleven of the twenty occupations projected to grow the fastest are related to health care and care of the elderly. This growth reflects the increased demand for health care by our aging population.

The health care industry, especially the nursing profession, is one of a handful of professions in which the number of openings far exceeds the number of qualified workers. This means your chances of getting a job after graduation and earning an above-average income are almost guaranteed. Very few industries can say that in today's world. The rest of the story is that you can find a job just about anywhere, and job security is unbeatable. You may work full time or part time and for as long as you like (assuming your skills remain intact). In many cases, your employer will offer you a sign-on bonus, and most will pay for all or part of your education if you choose to continue on for an advanced degree. In addition, there are a variety of job opportunities available ranging from direct patient care in hospitals, clinics, and nursing homes, home care and outpatient care, to patient care services such as patient transportation, record keeping, administration, sales, and medical supply.

The potential for fraud, security breaches, identity theft, and other forms of corporate or financial abuse will create new opportunities for accountants, auditors, investigators, lawyers, paralegals, and cyber security personnel. Gaming surveillance officers and gaming investigators are listed as one of the fastest-growing occupations for 2006 to 2016.

The *Business–Higher Education Forum* has projected that our nation will need more than 280,000 secondary math and science teachers by 2015.[17] Opportunities for adult education will continue as Americans continue learning and updating their skills through distance learning as well as traditional forms of higher education. Because of rapid technological changes in the computer and information technology fields, there will continue to be a need for individuals in these fields to train and retrain. Therefore, the information technology field should continue to offer many opportunities for qualified teachers. In addition, because of low numbers of doctoral candidates in the math and sciences and anticipated retirements of college faculty, many disciplines are facing shortages of professors. The most notable are in the math, science, nursing, and engineering fields.

According to data from the Bureau of Labor Statistics, service-providing industries will account for more than three quarters of all jobs in 2016.[18] Service-providing industries include *educational services* (schools and colleges), *financial services* (finance, insurance, real estate, and rental services), *health care and social assistance* (hospitals, clinics, assisted living, counseling services), *information* (publishing firms, movie, video, and sound production, broadcasting and telecommunications, information and data processing providers), *leisure and hospitality* (hotels, restaurants, sports, parks, performing arts companies), *professional and business services* (temporary help firms, consulting services, waste management establishments), *public administration* (federal, state, and local government), and *trade, transportation, and utilities* (wholesale and retail trade, airports, messenger services, and power plants). Among industries producing goods (construction, farming, mining, manufacturing), construction is projected to increase, whereas manufacturing is expected to decline.

The top five jobs to stay away from because of projected declines in employment are stock clerks and order fillers, cashiers (except gaming cashiers), packers and packagers, file clerks, and farmers and ranchers. The number of new jobs offered in telemarketing and computer operation is even expected to decline.

The need for technical work will continue to grow as technology changes and we become part of an increasingly global economy. Fewer young people are electing to pursue careers in engineering, science, and technology. This is a major concern for the U.S. because, without advances in these fields, most of our new products and new technologies cannot be developed. Job opportunities in science and engineering fields are wide open, especially for women and minorities, and will continue to be so for many years. Currently, there are shortages of mathematicians, scientists, engineers, auto mechanics, and HVAC technicians.

Although the manufacturing industry has been decimated by foreign competition, those manufacturers that do survive will continue to offer some of the highest wages for blue collar workers. There will be a continuing need for tool and die workers, machinists, and skilled workers familiar with manufacturing injection and blow molded plastic products. Other occupations that are expected to remain strong are the trucking industry, funeral services, and the construction industry. The need to repair our aging highways and bridges will continue to create a demand for civil engineers, engineering technicians, surveyors, heavy equipment operators, and laborers.

More recently, the outsourcing of not only manufacturing jobs but of *knowledge* worker jobs has become commonplace. Customer service centers, help desks, software development, income tax form preparation, book publishing and editing, financial and legal research, engineering and architectural design, and research have all become more economical to be performed in countries where wages are much lower than in the U.S. To safeguard ourselves against losing our jobs to outsourcing, it may be wise to choose an occupation that *cannot* be outsourced, in other words, any occupation that provides a direct service to people or requires that someone be physically present to perform the job or deliver the service. Occupations such as auto repair, construction, health care and medical treatment, education, food preparation, radio and television production, real estate, security, government, banking, cleaning and maintenance services, music, art, theatre, or home and backyard design are generally considered to be more outsource-proof than others. Even among some of the industries being sent overseas such as computer programming, there are still pockets of jobs within the larger industry that are more outsource-proof. Examples are web application programmers, networking managers, database developers, security experts, systems specialists, and onsite help desk specialists.

Today, we need to be more vigilant than ever for economic changes and how they may affect our careers. It wasn't too long ago that banking was considered a highly stable career. Today, competition, mergers, and acquisitions continue to shake up the industry and cause many bankers to lose jobs. Problems in one industry usually affect other industries. A good example is the recent mortgage crisis. As lenders tighten up their lending policies because of the increased number of foreclosures, this will make it more difficult for both businesses and consumers to get new loans. Subsequently, this will mean a reduction in new construction, which will result in fewer construction workers being hired. Less construction will impact building product manufacturers, retailers and distributors, insurance carriers, title insurance companies, real estate agents, mortgage bankers, and home improvement and furniture retailers.[19] Architects, lawyers, and surveyors who depend on new construction will also feel the trickle-down effects of the mortgage lending decline and must turn their attention to acquiring another type of clientele.

Some careerists have suggested we should *expect* that job change happens and prepare ourselves accordingly, that, by viewing our jobs as a series of *temporary assignments*, we may be in a better mindset to cope with change.

Despite what you have just read, the outlook is not all gloom and doom. On a positive note, the good news is that there will be more opportunities for skilled workers in the future, despite age or gender. Employers will adopt a more balanced view of work and its importance in relation to our personal, spiritual, and physical lives. There will be more flexible options available to workers regarding their daily work schedule, physical work setting, and more opportunities for part-time, temporary, home-based, or freelance work assignments.

Employers often cite their concern for the lack of "soft skills" in new graduates. This is an area in which more mature workers, who have been well schooled in customer service, telephone etiquette, and a good old-fashioned work ethic, will have the advantage over younger workers. As technology advances, there will be an emphasis on continuing to learn and grow, which will create more opportunities for personal and intellectual challenges and growth that will keep us all younger and working longer.

Chapter 2

Assess Your Present Situation

Success is not the key to happiness. Happiness is the key to success. If you love what you are doing, you will be successful.

Albert Schweitzer

What is your current employment or career situation? Have you recently been laid off or downsized? Do you need to find a new profession because of an accident or injury? Are you a single parent trying to find a better way to support yourself and your children? Do you want to get back into the workforce after staying home to raise your children? Or are you just looking for a career or job change? Whatever your particular situation, each of you faces a unique set of challenges, issues, and concerns. Some of you may have to make some relatively quick decisions about the best course of action to take, whereas others can take more time to digest the situation. This chapter will discuss each type of employment situation and identify and prioritize the immediate needs for each. Knowing what you have to do immediately and what can wait until another day is not only smart from a survival standpoint but will give you a greater sense of control over your life and your situation.

RECENTLY UNEMPLOYED OR DOWNSIZED

Finding out that your company has gone out of business or your department has been downsized is difficult to deal with, to say the least. Not only are you still reeling from the shock of losing your job, but you are faced with the task of trying to find another job that will hopefully pay as much as the one you had. Your days are probably filled with union meetings and presentations from human resources staff regarding severance packages, retirement options, and various outplacement programs and options. Added to that is the underlying anxiety of knowing that you only have a short period of time to find a new job before your unemployment benefits run out.

Finances are probably the number one priority for you at this time. Make sure you know what kind, if any, of severance pay or package you will be receiving. Will your company provide you with a letter of recommendation? Is your company offering any outplacement services such as classes, workshops, resume and cover letter preparation, or help finding a job?

If you haven't done so already, meet with a tax accountant, retirement specialist, unemployment representative, or some other financial professional. It may be possible to remortgage your home, take out a loan, cash in stocks or insurance policies, or negotiate with creditors regarding payment options.

Research and calculate the amount of severance pay or retirement package you'll receive, how long your unemployment benefits will last, and what other outplacement services your company has to offer to determine your "window" for finding another job, starting your own business, or going back to school for retraining. Keep in mind that if you were laid off from a company that moved its operations overseas, you may be eligible for Trade Act Assistance (TAA) benefits. TAA benefits will allow you to go back to school for two years to retrain for another career while retaining your unemployment benefits.

If you are the primary breadwinner in your family, you will need to determine the economic impact your lost job will have on yourself and your family, which will, in some ways, dictate your next course of action.

Review the following list. Add or delete items as necessary. Think about which items or tasks need to be attended to immediately and which ones can wait a week, a month, or even a year from now.

- Cash flow to pay bills and expenses
- Restructuring my finances
- Signing up for unemployment benefits
- Finding temporary employment
- Finding permanent employment
- Starting my own business
- Learning about retirement
- Changing my career
- Going back to school
- Other (describe)

List your top three immediate priorities:

1. _____
2. _____
3. _____

FORCED TO FIND A NEW CAREER BECAUSE OF DISABILITY

Are you a hairdresser who has suddenly developed carpal tunnel syndrome? Or a construction worker who can no longer do heavy lifting because of a bad back? Or perhaps you were a painter who fell from a ladder and can no longer stand for long periods of time? Work-related injury isn't something that only happens to older workers; it happens to workers of all ages and occurs in any type of occupation where physical injury or wear and tear on the body is a possibility. Those in agriculture, construction, general labor, and heavy equipment operation, as well as those who work as cashiers, computer operators, and secretaries, suffer from falls, machine accidents, muscle and back injury, and repetitive-motion related injuries like carpal tunnel syndrome.

For those of you who can no longer physically continue in your job or profession because of injury or an accident, your situation is similar to someone who's about to lose his or her job in that you will need to find a new source of employment. However, you have the added complication of your compromised health. First and foremost, your priority is to heal from your injuries and, through rehabilitation, regain as much of your former physical or mental functioning as possible. Unfortunately, along with the healing process come doctor visits, surgeries, physical, speech, or psychological therapy, and the mountains of paperwork involved in filing disability claims.

Once your physical condition has improved to the point where a prognosis can be made about your ability to return to work, then deciding which type of work to return to becomes the pressing issue. Start by talking with your human resources department at work or even an attorney if it becomes necessary to determine the timeline and dollar amount of any workers' compensation or sick time disability benefits for which you may qualify.

If you are lucky enough to work for a large company, it may be possible to move to a different job within the company and still keep your salary and benefits package (e.g., move to a desk job instead of being on the warehouse floor). Inquire about flexible work options and your employer's policies on their use. Investigate the possibility of transferring to another department or applying for another position within the company.

Talk with your employer or your human resources department about those options and how those changes may affect your pay and benefits. The state of your physical health, your skills and experience, level of education, and any resulting physical limitations will determine the extent to which remaining at your current place of employment will be possible. After gathering some facts, write up a formal proposal that explains how the new work arrangement will operate and what its advantages are for both you and your employer. Be sure to review any documents with your lawyer before submitting them to your employer.

If staying with your current employer is not an option, then the next step is to investigate the possibility of finding a different type of employment that will allow you to work within your physical limitations and still support yourself. Keep in mind that a career change may involve going back to school to upgrade your skills or earn the proper degree or certification. Meet with a vocational counselor from the Office of Vocational Rehabilitation to see if you qualify for any educational benefits that would allow you to train for a new profession.

Use your rehabilitation time to research and determine the best course of action for your particular situation. Meet with a career counselor, career coach, or disability specialist to help you plan out a future course of action. Take the time to think about what you want to do in the future and explore the kind of work that will best suit your interests, skills, and needs. Make an appointment to speak with admissions and financial aid representatives from your local college or university to determine what would be involved in returning to school, if necessary. Any income received from disability insurance benefits or Social Security will factor heavily into the equation.

Some of the issues you may be faced with include:

- Finances
- Applying for the appropriate medical or disability benefits
- Physical rehabilitation or any resulting health/medical issues
- Finding a new job
- Making a career change
- Career exploration
- Going back to school to retrain for a new career
- Taking time to decide what you want to do regarding job or career choice
- Other (describe)

List your top three immediate priorities:

1. _____

2. _____

3. _____

SINGLE PARENT

If you are a single parent who is considering going back to work or is looking for a better job, you have a unique set of challenges. Single parents have been described as "having twice the responsibility but only half the income." There are struggles of balancing work and the home responsibilities of raising children, not to mention scheduling some free time for your own needs. Financial security and finding affordable daycare for your children are usually among the biggest concerns. Filling the roles of both father and mother are full-time jobs in and of themselves. Every facet of your life may feel like a juggling act. Your life is about trying to do it all: taking care of the kids, holding down a job, making the meals, carpooling to and from daycare or after-school activities, fixing the leaky toilet, cleaning the house, and managing the budget.[1]

The goal of many single mothers and fathers is financial security. Because many are caught in low-paying jobs or are unemployed, they may decide to go back to school to prepare for a career that will provide a better life for themselves and their children. If you do not have a high school diploma or a GED, consider earning one. There are many free or low-cost GED study programs throughout the country that offer courses, study programs, testing sites, and even follow-up help with career or educational planning and help finding a job. The lack of a high school education will seriously limit your ability to find anything beyond a minimum wage job. Also, consider taking advantage of any community or federal assistance programs or services provided by community organizations that can help subsidize housing, transportation, daily living costs, and childcare. Don't let pride stand in your way. These programs are there to help you.

Review the following possible list of priorities:

- Earning a high school diploma or GED
- Budgeting
- Long-term financial security
- Affordable childcare

- Balancing home and work responsibilities
- Taking care of yourself mentally, physically, socially, and spiritually
- Finding a new or better job
- Changing careers
- Going back to school for a new career
- Other (describe)

What are your immediate needs?

1. _____
2. _____
3. _____

CHANGE IN MARITAL STATUS

If you are newly divorced (or about to divorce) or have recently lost your spouse, you have probably found yourself in the uncomfortable position of having to find a way to support yourself and your children by yourself. Perhaps you are a parent whose children are old enough to be in school during the day and you have decided to resume the job or career you had before your children were born. Your task is not as simple as just going out and getting another job. There are multiple things to consider and coordinate: writing a new resume, looking for job openings, deciding whether to go back part time or full time, lining up daycare or a babysitter for your children, and figuring out how to juggle work and family responsibilities.

If you are newly divorced or widowed and have spent the past several years staying at home to raise your children and manage the household, it has probably been many years since you last worked, not to mention attended school. Hopefully, you have obtained the services of a good attorney, legal advocate, or financial specialist. Prioritize your needs in order of importance and then work on developing short-term and long-term goals. For example, if your first priority is to get back into work force as quickly as possible, then your immediate goal will be to create a resume and begin the job search process. However, your long-term goal may be to go back to school and finish your teaching degree once your son or daughter begins elementary school. You will want to research the cost of finishing your degree and work with your attorney to negotiate a settlement that will include these costs.

If your circumstances are such that you do not immediately have to find work, you may be faced with making decisions about what to do with the rest of your life, personally and professionally. These may be issues you have not had to deal with before, but take comfort in knowing that there are many people and resources (including this book) available to help you move through the process.

Some of your issues and priorities may include:

- Legal issues
- Social services or mental health assistance
- Finances
- Childcare
- Finding a job
- Going back to school
- Taking time to plan for and make decisions about the rest of your life
- Other (describe)

List your top three immediate priorities:

1. _____
2. _____
3. _____

What are your next three priorities?

1. _____
2. _____
3. _____

LOOKING FOR A CAREER CHANGE

If you are considering looking for another job, there is probably something about your current work situation that is making you unhappy. Your issues are to identify *why* you are unhappy, whether or not you *should* leave, and *what* to do next.

People make the decision to change jobs for a variety of reasons: for advancement, prestige, a challenge, autonomy, new geographic location, more money, or because of boredom, stress, too many hours, too much travel, personality conflicts among bosses or coworkers, or because they are simply not making enough money to make ends meet. Although all of these situations will ultimately result in leaving a job, it is the *reasons* or the motivation behind the desire to leave that are worth investigating because they will contribute to your happiness or unhappiness in your next position.

It is also important to identify the underlying causes for your unhappiness at work to be able to find a new work situation that is more satisfying than the one you left. Use your negative feelings about work to guide you in identifying what is distasteful, bothersome, stressful, unfulfilling, boring, or problematic at work. What are the emotional or physiologic symptoms you are feeling as a result of your work? These are clues as to what is wrong. Use your feelings as a guide, but then use your brain to specifically identify what is contributing to your desire to leave.

Complete the following exercise and write down your answers on a separate sheet of paper:

- What do you like about your current job? Why?
- What do you dislike about your current job? Why?
- How are these problems affecting you?
- If you could change something about your job, what would it be?
- What would it feel like to have a job that you really enjoyed? How would your life be different?
- What do you need to have in a job to make you feel valued, satisfied, motivated, challenged, successful, or happy?
- Are there any outside circumstances or factors in your personal life that are contributing to your unhappiness at work?

Rank your priorities in order of importance:

___Finding a different job

___Changing careers

___Going back to school

___Starting my own business

___Cutting back hours or working part time

___Discovering what I want to do with my life

___Learning something new or developing a hobby

___Improving the physical, emotional, spiritual, or social aspects of my life

___Other (describe)

Knowing what you can and cannot control in your work situation will also help you determine whether leaving your job is the best solution. For example, if the issue is too much work or too many hours, is your workload something that you can adjust (by talking with your boss and negotiating a more reasonable workload, hiring an additional staff member, delegating work to others, or by working more efficiently)? Or is your workload beyond your control (a function of the company's philosophy or administrative structure, financial difficulties, the management style of your employer, or the nature of your occupation)? If you have determined that there is no way to create a more manageable workload, then leaving may be the best possible solution. However, if the reason for your unmanageable workload has more to do with your personal work style than the company you work for (e.g., inability to say no to clients, taking on too much responsibility, inability to prioritize tasks), then not recognizing these factors will result in carrying these work traits to the next job where you will eventually end up creating another unmanageable workload situation.

Midlife is often the time when we begin to re-evaluate our lives, our relationships, and our work. Is our work fulfilling, or is it physically and emotionally draining? Often, we assume that we're unhappy because something is missing from our life, whereas the opposite may be true. We may be experiencing *too much* of something, like too many hours, or too much travel, or too much customer interaction, which prevents us from enjoying a work activity we would otherwise enjoy if we did it for fewer hours or with some breaks in between.

Take the time now to address some larger life-related questions:

- What do you want out of life? (goals, aspirations, wishes)
- What would it take to achieve those goals or to improve your life?
- What does work mean to you and how does it fit into your life?
- What is your dream job/career/occupation?
- How would your job help you achieve your goals or make your life more enjoyable?
- What could be accomplished immediately?
- What could be accomplished within the next 1 to 4 years?
- What could be accomplished in 5 to 10 years?

Although you may be feeling some urgency to leave your job, don't act on those feelings yet. You might have more options open to you *because* you are employed than if you were unemployed. Remaining employed for a little while longer will give you the time you need to reflect upon your situation, examine each of your options, and make a career move that will allow you to create a brighter and more satisfying future.

EMPLOYED, BUT NOT MAKING A LIVING

Are you employed at a job that you enjoy but find you can barely pay the bills on what you bring home each week? Is it true that even though you recently received a pay raise, the cost of health care premiums, prescription copays, gas, food, rent, and just about everything else around you has also gone up until it seems like you're getting further and further behind? Perhaps you're thinking about starting a family, or are already a parent whose children are getting older, and you suddenly realize that you're going to need to find a job that pays better and offers more benefits to support a family and provide them with a decent living environment. You may also be one of the many Americans who have the additional financial burden of supporting parents or grandchildren or are temporarily helping out siblings, nieces, or nephews while they're in between jobs.

Like the career changer, *because* you are still employed, you have the advantage of being able to plan a strategy to improve your financial situation while still drawing a paycheck. Making plans now to improve your financial situation will allow you to earn enough money in the near future to create the type of life you want for yourself and your family. Your immediate priority is to do everything you can to cut down on excess spending and apply for any assistance programs you might qualify for. The next steps are to carefully research the marketplace, itemize your job skills, and determine whether searching for a new job or enrolling in school is going to be the best option for your particular situation. Unless you have the education and work experience to immediately move into a better paying position, you will need to invest some time in obtaining the skills and educational credentials needed to improve your situation—unless you suddenly win the lottery. Hmm, maybe playing the lottery isn't such a bad idea.

Rank your priorities in order of importance:

___Budgeting or restructuring my finances

___Increasing cash flow or source of income

___Credit counseling or debt management

___Finding a different job

___Starting my own business

___Changing careers

___Earning the degree or credentials to qualify for a better job

___Balancing work and family

___Other (describe)

Chapter 3

Deal with Common Emotions

It's not whether you get knocked down, it's whether you get up.

Vince Lombardi

Whatever your particular reason for wanting to reenter the job market, you are probably experiencing uncertainly, apprehension, and a considerable amount of anxiety about your situation. Rest assured that what you are feeling is perfectly normal and would be experienced by anyone in your situation.

Why is work such a big deal? And why are we so affected by a change in our work status? The answer is because work is such an integral part of our lives. We spend more time working than we do anything else in our lives, and, as a culture, we place more value on our success in the workplace than our success at home. Although the extent to which we define ourselves through our work varies by individual, for many of us, especially men, work is *who* and *what* we are. Work provides structure to our day, gives us something to brag or complain about, and provides a connection with others in our community. Work dissatisfaction and burnout have been found to lead to depression and anxiety and will often spill over to nonwork relationships and situations. Work can make us feel stimulated, competent, successful, and powerful, or it can make us feel bored, tired, used, and abused. Work can be a place of social support and comfort, or a way to avoid people and escape from stressful situations or unhappy experiences. In other words, work "works" both ways.

PAST DECISIONS, FUTURE QUANDARIES

It's easy at this point in your life to look back and say, "I should have left my job years ago," or, "I wish I'd gone to college right after high school," or,

"Imagine what my life would be like today if only I had done such and such." It's easy to second-guess decisions with the advantage of hindsight. Granted, some of the decisions you have to make now may not have existed if you'd made different choices when you were graduating from high school. But then again, I doubt that you are the same person today that you were five, ten, or twenty years ago, and your priorities and personal circumstances are probably much different today than what they were back then. People generally make the best decisions they can at the time. Learn from your experience and move on.

RECENTLY UNEMPLOYED

If you've been downsized, right-sized, bought out, outsourced, or have just simply found yourself out of a job, you are probably feeling a mixture of anger, panic, disillusionment, helplessness, and a sense of betrayal. Most people are emotionally unprepared for job loss and find it devastating when it does happen. Even if you suspected you were going to be laid off from work, it was probably still quite a blow when it actually happened.

After the shock of losing your job wears off, you may begin experiencing a variety of emotions and may even feel like you're riding an emotional roller coaster.[1] Many experts compare the emotional effects of job loss with a grief reaction, and you may experience a sequence of stages until the loss is resolved. The stages of loss or grief include

- Shock, you are not fully aware of what just happened
- Denial, you cannot believe that the company laid you off
- Relief, you may feel like a burden has been lifted
- Anger, you blame those you think might be responsible, including yourself
- Depression, it may set in when you comprehend the reality of the situation
- Acceptance, the final stage of the process when you come to terms with your unemployment and are able to move beyond it.[2]

Unfortunately, when a layoff happens, employees are often notified in a large group forum and are then channeled through a series of company-sponsored outplacement services to help them make a decision about their future. The problem is that most employees are asked to make significant decisions about their future without the necessary time to process what has just happened. Many of the individuals I see need to make a relatively quick decision about whether to go back to school or find another job. Many, however, are still in the midst of the shock, anger, or depression stages of their grief. Ideally, the "acceptance" stage is the place to be when determining what you want to do with the rest of your work life. Unfortunately, many displaced employees simply do not have the luxury of waiting until they reach this point. Of course, it is possible to make good decisions and function during the earlier stages of grief, but you need to be very aware of how your emotions are influencing the decisions you have to make.

The uncertainty about your future, the worry over paying your bills and meeting family responsibilities and obligations, as well as the physical and emotional stress of searching for a new job can lead to fatigue, depression, anxiety, irritability, headaches, muscle pain, stomach problems, and a myriad of other stress-related symptoms. It is important to take care of yourself physically, mentally, and spiritually during this time. If you start to see yourself engaging in angry or depressive thoughts or behaviors on a daily basis, then it's time to get some professional help and support.

If you find yourself unable to stop rehashing the circumstances that led up to your unemployment, here's a simple, but effective, thought-stopping technique. Force yourself to limit the time you spend thinking about how you lost your job to, say, five or ten minutes. Set the buzzer on your watch or other electronic device, and when the buzzer goes off, stop, physically get up, and go do something else. Writing your thoughts down on paper will also help. Keep a log, blog, or journal of your feelings. The process of writing or blogging will often interrupt the flow of internal chatter that can churn around inside your head. Try to counter your negative thoughts with positive ones. If you focus on what you can do, and remind yourself about the positive aspects of your life, you will end up feeling a whole lot better about yourself and your situation.

I think the hardest part about being unemployed is enduring the time between losing your job and finding a new one. It is sometimes extremely difficult to remain optimistic during this period of time, but that's exactly what you must do. Try to spend some time each day doing something productive—this will not only help you regain a sense of control over your life but will help pass the time.

The following are suggestions of what to do when you are laid off:

1. Take advantage of any and all company-sponsored workshops, employment assistance or outplacement programs, severance pay, and early retirement options.
2. Talk with an accountant, financial planner, credit counselor, and your local unemployment office. Know what your severance pay will be and

how long your benefits will last. Find out if you qualify for unemployment benefits, retraining programs, or any kind of state or federal financial aid, tuition assistance, scholarships, or loans.

3. Call a family meeting to discuss the situation with your partner or spouse and children. Don't try to shoulder your problems all by yourself. Remember that your family is affected by all of this too, and you may be surprised how resourceful and supportive your family can be if you let them.

4. Review and revise your monthly living expenses. Cut down on costs if you need to. Talk to your creditors, lenders, or your bank about reducing monthly payments or arranging special payment plans. Find ways to save money or raise extra cash during your unemployment through freelancing, consulting, or registering with a temporary help service.

5. If you have children attending college, schedule an appointment with the college's financial aid office to discuss your situation and make the appropriate adjustments to your child's financial aid package.

6. Avoid isolation. Keep in touch with your friends and even your former coworkers if you used to see each other socially. Many unemployed individuals often feel a sense of loneliness and isolation because they miss the daily interaction with people at work. It is important to get out of the house and interact with people. Schedule phone calls, luncheon dates, or plan activities such as going to a concert or sporting event, working out at the gym or recreation center, volunteering to go on a field trip with your child's class, etc.

7. Get plenty of rest, exercise, nutrition, and relaxation to counter the effects of stress and provide you with the energy needed to deal with this situation.

8. Consider joining a support group to find help and understanding from people who are going through or have gone through a similar experience. If your depression won't go away, or you find yourself excessively using alcohol or drugs to feel better, you may wish to consider seeking professional counseling services.

The current research on *resiliency*, which is the ability to bounce back from major life-changing events, shows that resilient individuals are able to take major life-altering events and circumstances and turn them around into better, stronger opportunities.[3] Use your emotions to propel you into action and use that energy to capitalize on any new opportunities that might arise from your job loss.

Remember that everyone reacts to change in different ways and heals from trauma at their own rate. Although there are general stages of grief that people go through, there is no set timeline for recovery. It is important to recognize that what you are feeling is perfectly normal and will get better with time.

FORCED TO FIND A NEW JOB OR CAREER

According to the U.S. Department of Labor, Occupational Safety and Health Administration (OSHA), repetitive strain injuries are the nation's most common and costly occupational health problem, affecting hundreds of thousands of American workers and costing more than $20 billion a year in workers' compensation.[4] Repetitive strain injuries commonly affect the wrist, elbow, or shoulder. Only 23% of all carpal tunnel syndrome patients actually returned to their previous professions after surgery.

I have worked with a number of former cosmetologists who had to give up their profession because the years of stress on their arms and backs from standing on their feet and raising their arms to cut hair had taken their toll. Likewise, I have spoken with former construction workers, painters, and laborers who needed to find new careers that did not involve standing, bending, or lifting because of knee and back injuries.

For those of you who can no longer physically continue in your job or profession because of injury or an accident, your emotional reactions are going to be similar to the person who has suddenly been laid off because you have experienced a sudden, unexpected termination from your career. However, unlike the person who has been laid off, you do not have the option of continuing your former job at a new place of employment.

You will have to find a new job or profession, which essentially forces you to reinvent yourself. As you go through this process and come to terms with the loss of your profession, you may find it difficult to let go of old expectations and find something new to get excited about. First, explore the possibility of returning to your former job or profession in a different role. Many athletes become teachers or coaches. Explore the possibility of becoming a supervisor, manager, owner, teacher, trainer, or researcher. If it is not possible to remain in your current profession, think of this as an opportunity to do something new or pursue a career or interest that you never had the opportunity to do before.

In addition to coming to terms about the loss of your profession, you are also dealing with the physical aspects of your injury or disability. There are the added complications of going through physical rehabilitation, doctor visits, surgeries, and mountains of paperwork. There are also the issues of dealing with chronic pain, loss of mobility, fear of re-injury, lack of independence, and the unfamiliar reliance upon others to help you do the things you used to do on your own.

It is not uncommon for family interactions to become strained as everyone struggles to adjust and adapt to their new roles. Dad may be home more while mom works. Family tensions may arise, brought on by the frustration of having to rely on a spouse, child, or relative to drive you to doctor appointments or assume some of the chores and other responsibilities around the house that you used to do. If you are dealing with an injury, you may be experiencing the debilitating effects of chronic pain that interrupts sleep, hinders decision-making, affects your personality, and limits your productivity. You are learning to adjust to life and your family in a new way, and feelings of anger, frustration, and sadness are common reactions to the grief and emotional aspects of your disability or injury.

When people are out of work for a period of time, it is easy for them to lose touch with people and become isolated. Just as when people retire, they find themselves missing the interaction they had with people during the day and feel isolated and bored sitting at home. Action and social interaction are the antidotes to boredom, isolation, and depression. Try to keep in touch with your friends through lunch, sports activities, or other social visits and outings. Research has shown that chronic pain alone can lead to depression and thoughts of suicide.[5] So be sure to rehab your mood as well as your body. And, above all, be kind to yourself and take advantage of any available support systems as you need them. Here are some suggested activities to help you through the process:

1. Talk to your employer or human resources department about the possibility of transferring to a different department within your company.

2. Apply for Social Security disability benefits or workers' compensation, if appropriate.

3. Get the proper medical treatment and continue with any physical therapy and pain management treatment as needed.

4. Seek mental health support and therapy if you are feeling overly angry, frustrated, depressed, or suicidal. Counseling can help you deal with the issues of job loss as well as any family relationship difficulties.

5. Schedule regular visits with friends and engage in hobbies (or develop new ones). Try to get out of the house at least once a day if only to take a walk or drive around the block. Volunteer to help a neighbor or a nonprofit organization a few hours a week.

6. Meet with a career counselor or job coach to help you brainstorm ways to remain in your profession in a new capacity or develop a new career interest.

HATE YOUR JOB?

Do you dread Monday mornings? Are you bored, stressed out, or just simply dislike your job? Is your boss driving you nuts? Do the hours creep by at an ungodly slow pace each day?

You may even be saying things to yourself like, "I can't wait to go home," or you may be feverishly playing the lottery in hopes of winning your chance to freedom. But freedom to do what? How you answer that question may provide clues to your next course of action.

No matter how much you hate your job, take a deep breath and resist the tendency to quit your job. The grass is not necessarily greener on the other side! Don't compound an unbearable situation by adding the financial pressures of not being able to pay bills because of lost income. The last thing you want to do is find yourself in a situation where you are forced to jump right back into another job you don't like simply because you're unemployed. Take the time now, while you're still drawing a paycheck, to reflect on your life and think about what you'd like to do in the future. Then develop a plan to transition into that new future.

I once worked with a young woman in her early thirties who absolutely hated her job. She desperately wanted out, but when she looked at the want ads she became discouraged because they didn't pay as much as she was currently making. She became so confused and frustrated that she couldn't even think straight. Luckily, she didn't just up and leave her job. After getting past some of the emotion, she was able to look at her situation a little more objectively and took the time to analyze what it was about her situation that made her so upset. Although she was in a position that bored her to tears, it turned out that the underlying issue was the fear that she would be "stuck" in a boring, dead-end job without having a way out. Once she began to realize that she had other options, and she began to view her current position as a *temporary* work assignment rather than a reflection of her life and self-worth, she was able to explore options and focus on developing a strategy to improve her employment situation.

Take a thoughtful look at your situation and make a list of the good and bad aspects of your current job or position. Try to identify which factors you would like to change to have an "ideal" position and what you would like to retain. If you are having trouble deciding what to do in this next stage of your life or are unsure about your career choices, consider making an appointment with a career counselor or career coach.

If your job is tolerable and you're making a decent salary, but work's just not doing it for you, then maybe something else is missing in your life. A job can't fill all the voids. Maybe your life situation is different now, or your values have changed from when you began your career. Would starting a new hobby, going on a vacation, entering a new relationship, or getting a pet make your life better? Try to identify what's missing or, better yet, try to come up with answers to the question, "What would it take to make my life better?" Another way to ask the same question is, "What would my life look like if it were happy and fulfilling?" Think about, in vivid detail, how your life would be and then write those details down on a piece of paper or type it out on your laptop. These are not quick, five-minute answers; they deal with complex life issues that involve determining who you are, what you want to become, and where you fit in the world. The answers to these questions may require a substantial amount of time, reflection, and thought. Consider discussing the matter with a trusted friend or a career counselor, psychologist, or spiritual advisor.

The following are some suggestions of what to do in the meantime:

1. Complete a career interest inventory and engage in reflective thought about your interests, goals, values, and future dreams.

2. Visit (online or in person) colleges or universities in your area to see what they have to offer.

3. Make an appointment with a career counselor or job coach.

4. Create a one-year, five-year, and ten-year educational or career plan.

5. Talk to friends, neighbors, family members, or acquaintances about their jobs (also called informational interviewing).

6. Research the marketplace (but be careful about using the Internet at work to look for a new job). Use your vacation time to research new companies.

7. Take the time to redefine who you are or who you would want to be.

8. Try to find something enjoyable about your current position and spend some time each day doing that task.

9. Learn something new at work. Tackle a new software program, volunteer for an interesting assignment, or help a coworker out with a project. If your company offers tuition reimbursement, take a class, learn a language, or upgrade your skills.

10. Boost your nonwork life. Start a hobby, a relationship (or focus on the one you have), take a vacation, adopt a puppy, or join a club, play a sport, or get involved in a community project or cause. Focusing on other aspects of your life has a way of deemphasizing work.

SINGLE PARENT

Although single parents often feel isolated, there are approximately fourteen million single parents in the U.S. today, and the number of single parent families continues to grow.[6] Of these single parents, 83.1% are mothers and 16.9% are fathers.

Whether you are a single mother or father, raising children alone is a daunting task. All the childcare and financial responsibilities are on your shoulders. There is no one there to watch the kids while you work, fix the leaky faucet, or shovel snow from the driveway. If someone comes down with the flu at school, you are the one who must leave work to pick him or her up. You have become a master at coordinating, organizing, and budgeting. In a world where it takes two people and two incomes to raise and support a family, anyone who can successfully raise their children alone deserves a standing ovation (and a quiet vacation in Hawaii).

Here are some suggestions for what to do if you are one of these parents:

1. Investigate the possibility of going back to school either to earn your degree or to retrain for a new career. If you have never earned a high school diploma, take classes to prepare for your GED examination. If you have a GED or high school diploma, consider going to college to earn an associate or bachelor's degree. Having a degree will greatly increase your earning power.

2. Check with your local One-Stop Career Center for help in locating any sources of financial assistance for displaced homemakers or single parents returning to school as well as assistance for childcare costs. Also, check with your local college or university to see if they offer any state or federally funded grant programs that will provide financial or academic assistance for GED holders, single parents, or displaced homemakers.

3. Make an appointment with a career or vocational counselor at your local college, university, or One-Stop Career Center to help with preparing a resume, applying for jobs, or deciding which career to pursue.

4. Enlist the help of family members, friends, or any other community-based support groups to help you handle the responsibilities of raising a family by yourself. Family and friends may be willing to help out with baby-sitting. Manage what you can as efficiently as possible and try to delegate the rest. Consider joining a support group for single parents. Many groups have play groups, baby-sitting pools, and social activities that the whole family can participate in. If there isn't an existing support group in your community, consider starting one.

5. Many single parents are so consumed by the daily tasks of taking care of their children that they neglect their own emotional needs. Try to be a "good enough" parent not a "perfect" one. Don't neglect your own social life and take a break when you become too emotionally exhausted. If you are feeling unusually stressed, angry, depressed, or overwhelmed by your situation, seek the services of a professional counselor. Being a good single parent means knowing how to take care of yourself and relax so you can "refuel" and have enough to give to your child.

6. Seek out help whenever you need it. There are many sources of help available in your community in addition to the help and advice received from neighbors, family, and friends. If your children are having difficulty at school, you can request help from school personnel; social services agencies can help with family issues or provide parenting information; state and local government agencies can provide financial and medical assistance if needed; and nationwide organizations for single parents can provide support and information.

7. Remember to do something fun each day with your children as well as for yourself. Try to enjoy the time you spend together because it is easy to become too focused on the daily job of trying to get everything done. Schedule fun activities that fit into your budget like going camping, taking a hike or going on a picnic, or going to the zoo or the movies.

8. Exhaustion is a common complaint for single parents, so take care of your physical needs by getting enough rest. Also, remember to engage in some kind of exercise and get the proper nutrition to refuel your body as well as your mind.

RECENTLY DIVORCED OR WIDOWED

Some of you may have made the decision to stay at home and raise your children. Now that your children are starting school, or are married with children of their own, it may be time to resume your career or go back to school to earn your degree. Or perhaps you recently lost your spouse or partner or are going through a divorce and must go back to work to support yourself.

Whatever the circumstance, you are probably feeling hurt, angry, scared, and overwhelmed. Many of the women I have worked with feel directionless and at a loss with what to do next with their lives. Others struggle with deep feelings of anger. One woman remarked, "I spent the last twenty years raising my children and running a household. I quit college to help support *him* through his career. We had it all planned, the trips, the vacation house after retirement ... now this happened and here I am starting all over again."

Healing will take some time, and you should take advantage of any counseling services, support groups, pastoral services, or other supportive networks or systems in your community. In one sense, you're getting hit with a double whammy. Going back to work is a big change in and of itself, but equally challenging to overcome is the reason behind why you need to return to school or work.

If your pain or grief is too raw to allow you to think clearly, enlist the aid of a friend or professional to help you weigh decisions and explore options. Some people need time to regain the proper perspective before they can make any decision about their future. Others have to make a decision rather quickly because of divorce negotiations. Here are some suggestions for the transition:

1. Prioritize. Make a list of what you need to address today and what can wait until tomorrow, next week, or next month.

2. Seek the advice of a good lawyer, accountant, financial planner, college admissions counselor, career counselor/coach, or other counseling professional to help you through the process and make the best decisions for your particular situation.

3. Find out exactly what your financial situation is. If you have not done so already, establish a line of credit. Consider working part time or with a temporary help service to generate enough cash flow to pay bills until you find a full-time job or your settlement is finalized.

4. If you are considering resuming a former profession, check with your state's licensing or certification board to determine what will be needed to regain your credentials. Depending on the profession and the length of time you were away from work, you may need to return to school for retraining or refresher courses.

5. If you are considering going back to school to prepare for a particular occupation, make an appointment with a college admissions counselor, the financial aid office, and a career counselor or coach to discuss your educational and financial options. Then share this information with your lawyer or attorney to see if those educational costs can be included in your divorce settlement.

6. If your divorce or widowhood is fairly recent, your emotions may be too raw to make any major decisions about your future. Take the time

to discover who you are, outside of being a wife and mother, and what you want to do with your life.

7. Create a support group of people who can provide you with emotional support, advice, and encouragement.

8. Treat yourself to long walks in the park, a massage, a movie, eating out, a pedicure, shopping, and anything else that will make you feel pampered for an hour or so.

Try to be positive; please don't fall into the trap of thinking your time and life has been wasted. Instead, try to salvage the good memories. Consider what you have accomplished, such as raising a healthy family, having a wonderful relationship with your children, being active in your community, or running the family business without a degree. The skills you have used over the years will transfer into the workplace. The important thing to remember is that now it's time to do something for you, to spend your time, money, and resources on creating the kind of life and future you deserve.

JUST CAN'T MAKE A LIVING

You're working full time and have cut back on expenses as much as you can, but when payday rolls around, you barely have enough to pay the bills as the cost of groceries, fuel, and taxes increase. Perhaps you are even working two jobs just to make ends meet, and still you can't seem to get ahead. Financially, you feel like you are walking on quicksand, and some of you are beginning to feel trapped, discouraged, or depressed.

Underemployment is a real problem in today's economy, and one that is shared by many. Even though your income is inadequate, you are doing your part to support your family, and, from an employment standpoint, you are still in a better position to improve your situation than if you were unemployed. Take the time now to begin making plans to improve your financial situation.

Suggested activities while you're still working and waiting for a better opportunity include

1. Itemize your weekly, monthly, and yearly expenses. Balance your budget the best you can and talk to your electric, gas, water, garbage, or other utility companies about budgeting program plans that may allow you to spread out payments over the year. Apply for any low-income assistance programs that you may qualify for. Talk to your creditors about having mortgage, loans, or credit payments consolidated or

spread out to allow you to pay smaller monthly installments. Seek the assistance of an accountant, a free credit service, or other financial advisor to help you budget more efficiently or manage your debt.

2. Investigate the possibility of picking up extra hours, working overtime, or taking on a second job. Talk with your boss or your human resources office about the possibility of obtaining a raise, a promotion, or a transfer to a better-paying position within your company. If you are employed part time, find out what you need to do to become full time. What is the system for advancement at your company? Do you need experience, seniority, special skills, or more education? Once you identify what you need to do to advance, then you can begin implementing steps to obtain a better-paying position.

3. Research the marketplace (but be careful about using the Internet at work) to look for a new job. Where are the jobs in your area? Which ones are "hot" and which ones are cooling off? What majors or programs are offered at your local college or technical center? Which have the best placement rates or pay the best salary for the shortest amount of time in college? Ask your local chamber of commerce or One-Stop Career Center if they expect any new companies or industries to be moving into your community that might provide better jobs. Look up the salary and labor market trends and forecasts in your state or major metropolitan area.

4. Visit the colleges or universities in your area to see what kind of short-term credit, certificate, or continuing education programs they have to offer.

5. Make an appointment with a career counselor or job coach to discuss possible educational and career opportunities.

6. Actively research job openings. Are there other jobs that would pay more than you are now making? Are there any opportunities to supplement your income with part-time or seasonal work or a home- or Internet-based business?

WHILE YOU'RE LOOKING FOR A NEW JOB

Unfortunately, finding a new job just takes time. Depending on your local job market, it may take anywhere from three weeks to eight months to find a new position. To improve your chances of success, you should treat looking for a job as if it were a full-time job. That is, set up a daily schedule of looking for job openings, sending out your resume, and interviewing and networking with possible employers as if it were a job. The more actively involved you are in the process, the more interviews you'll have, which will increase the chances that one of those interviews will result in a job offer.

What makes searching for a new job emotionally difficult is the uncertainty and lack of control inherent in the process. We have no way of knowing when a new job will appear, or who our competition will be when we interview. Employers have their own timelines, needs, agendas, and personal preferences when it comes to selecting a candidate. Sometimes jobs are filled by internal candidates, or candidates are selected for reasons that have nothing to do with you. Put these realities into the proper perspective when you start getting down on yourself about not getting a job right away. All you can do is be persistent and continue to apply for jobs. If you were called in for an interview and didn't get the position, try to find out what you could have done to improve your chances. It may also help to go through some practice or "mock" interviews with friends or family members to polish your interviewing skills. The good news is that the more interviews you participate in, the better you will become at interviewing, which in and of itself will improve your chances of being hired. Learn from your experiences and keep plugging away. Think positively. Remember, it doesn't matter how many resumes you send out or how many applications you complete; you only need one job offer.

While you were working you were used to a daily routine. Try to regain that sense of normalcy by following some kind of routine or schedule. Adding some structure to your day will not only give you a sense of purpose but a feeling of accomplishment at the end of the day. Some people will even take on a volunteer position or a part-time job at a department store just to give them something to do. This not only brings in some extra cash, but, more importantly, it gives them a reason to get up and get dressed in the morning instead of sitting in front of the television in their pajamas all day. Getting out of the house is good for everyone, regardless of their employment situation, and talking with different types of people keeps you socially connected and increases the likelihood that you will hear about a new job opening. The following are suggestions for how to spend all that "free" time:

1. Set aside a period of time each day to search, apply for, and interview for jobs.

2. Spend time each day for exercise or relaxation to combat the effects of stress.

3. Take up a new hobby, learn to play an instrument, or take a class.

4. If money or funding allows, pick up some extra training that will make you more marketable, such as a computer class.

5. Volunteer at your local library, senior center, pet shelter, church bazaar, or hospital.

6. Don't forget to schedule time to do something fun with your partner or spouse, your children, your relatives, and your friends.

7. Offer to do some of the chores your partner or spouse usually does during the day like picking up the kids from soccer practice, doing the grocery shopping, making supper, or mowing the lawn.

Spend the free time you do have (it won't be there forever) in an enjoyable way. Take this time to learn something new, read that book that's been collecting dust on your nightstand, or go to that ball game you never had time to see before. If money is an issue, there are usually a variety of free or inexpensive activities offered through your community. Go for a walk, go swimming or ice skating (depending on the season), spend a day at the park, visit the zoo or a museum or an art festival, arrange a luncheon date, or attend the matinee showing of a movie or a play. Do something you enjoy each day. Remember, this is a temporary situation!

Chapter 4

Take Stock of What You Already Have

Success is to be measured not so much by the position that one has reached in life as by the obstacles which he or she has overcome.

Booker T. Washington

Job seekers often believe the first step in finding a job is to update their resumes. Although this is an important step in looking for a job, it is impossible to effectively market yourself when you don't know what you're selling. So, let's back up a step and determine what your assets are and how you want to use those assets in the job market.

You are made up of the sum of your collective experience. When it comes to work, we are made up of the sum of our educational background, our work experience, our hard skills (job-specific skills or knowledge), and our work-related social or personal skills, called *soft skills*.

Whether you're a receptionist or the CEO of a company, everyone has a set of skills. The difference is that each of us uses a different set of skills at a different level within the organization we work for. A secretary, for example, knows how to greet clients, answer the phone properly (i.e., placing callers on hold while picking up the next ringing line without losing the first caller), prepare charts, file, type a memo using Microsoft Word, and prepare a budget using an Excel spreadsheet. The CEO oversees the entire company's operations, manages the budget and generates a profit, responds to shareholders, and creates a favorable public image in the community. Each has a respective skill set with varying levels of responsibility.

TRANSFERABLE SKILLS

Transferable skills (sometimes called functional skills) are those work-related skills that can be *transferred* from one job to another. The stay-at-home mom, who organizes car pools and runs her son's little league fund-raising events, could transfer her "organizational" skills and "fund-raising" experience from little league to a position with a nonprofit organization as a volunteer. Likewise, chiropractors could transfer their knowledge of chiropractic medicine and experience in educating patients about proper musculoskeletal health to a teaching position in a college or university. Or they could apply their analytical and observational skills to the process of reviewing disability claims for an insurance company or the Social Security Administration.

There are limits to how much transferable skills will actually transfer. Some jobs will require a certain level of educational or industry knowledge that can only be gained through additional education or experience. Making the case for using transferable skills in the absence of industry experience only works if the jobs are related and share many of the same skill sets. An English teacher could easily make the transition to educational sales, become a book editor, a tour guide, or even a corporate trainer but would have a difficult time securing a job as a medical laboratory assistant (unless they formerly taught chemistry).

That being said, if you have little work experience, you have to draw upon what skills you do possess. So think about any committees you served on, or any volunteer, community, or nonprofit organizations you belonged to and any work you did while a member. Many of the activities done in these organizations are similar to paid work experiences. One year, I organized a craft fair for a local community organization. I organized volunteers and vendors, held meetings, prepared a budget, prepared publicity articles for the local newspaper, arranged for security, kept records, handled revenue, troubleshot problems, resolved customer complaints, answered questions, provided information, met deadlines, anticipated potential problems, and prayed for a nice, sunny day. When it was all over, I think I worked harder on this project than I did at my "real" job. So think about all of the events you were involved in during the past five years. If you managed a similar event on a volunteer or nonpaid basis, you can claim those skills as legitimate experience.

Obviously, some skills have broader applications than others. Writing, speaking, and selling skills can be broadly applied to a variety of different jobs, whereas programming in C++ is a specific skill that can only be applied to a computer programming position. However, the ability to use Microsoft Office (a collection of software programs common to many PCs) in an insurance office is a skill that can be easily transferred to a doctor's office or an administrative office at a university. In the latter case, moving from a secretary/receptionist position in a medical office to a university setting would be considered a "promotion" if the job title happened to be "executive secretary to the vice president of academic affairs."

YOUR EMPLOYABILITY PACKAGE

Try to look at all of your skills, education, and work experience as the package that you are trying to sell to a potential employer. Ask yourself what you have that an employer can use. This perspective will allow you to view yourself more objectively and will make it easier to market yourself. Your employability package is not only made up of your education, experience, skills, accomplishments, and strengths or areas of expertise but also your personal characteristics, your enthusiasm and ability to get along with others, your work ethic, and whether you are calm, creative, analytical, or spontaneous.

Skills are invisible to an employer. Interviewing candidates for a job is not like selling a house where the buyer can tour the rooms, check the basement for leaks, and determine the square footage of the backyard. That's why many employers are now relying on employee testing, asking behavioral based or situational questions in the interview, and requiring applicants to take a typing test before being hired. You must present your skills and attributes (employment package) in a way that verbally (interview) or visually (resume, cover letter, portfolio, web page) creates an image of what you have to offer. Think about how you want to be viewed by an employer and construct your presentation to transmit that image.

Some skills can be inferred from a job title, such as "computer programmer," but job seekers, and especially those changing careers, need to take a more active role in helping an employer connect the dots between their skills in their old job and the skills needed in the new job.

UNDERSTANDING HOW JOBS ARE CLASSIFIED

Most traditional companies are arranged in a top-down, pyramid-shaped hierarchy in which there are four distinct levels of responsibility: 1) labor (blue collar, service professions, and clerical), 2) professional staff (entry level positions designed for individuals with no or limited work experience), 3) management (executives, directors, managers, supervisors), and 4) executive (owners, CEOs, partners, chairman, president). These levels are based on skills, level of productivity, amount of responsibility, and authority. In general, individuals at the top have the most power and authority, whereas individuals in the bottom layers (who often outnumber those in the top layer) have less power and authority. Power and authority are tied to an individual's level of responsibility, ability to make decisions, degree of independence, or supervision of people or projects.

Each individual position in an organization is assigned a job title, description, and a grade level according to a variety of factors, such as where it fits into the organizational structure, the amount of responsibility and level of authority, who the position reports to or interacts with on a daily basis, the degree of independence, the number of people the position supervises, the consequence of a wrong decision or action, and the minimum amount of education, years of experience, and skills required to adequately perform those duties. The greater the skill level and the more responsibility and authority attached to the duties within a particular position, the more you are paid to do it. This is the basis of the classification system most human resource managers use to organize employees by job title, pay scales, rank, and grade levels within an organization.

When writing a resume, use action words that reflect the level of responsibility and skill of your position. Commonly used "action" words listed in resume guides, such as "directed," "coordinated," and "managed," are considered higher-level job functions than "filed" or "typed."

Many people mistakenly assume that if their workload increases, they should be paid more to do their job. But increasing the volume or amount of work doesn't necessarily mean that the level of responsibility or authority of the job has changed. It's just more of the same kind of work. That's why our secretary's "supervisor" has a higher job classification and as a result earns a higher salary.

COLLEGE MAJORS AND CAREERS

I often hear people say, "I've got three degrees and I still can't find a job," or, "I just graduated with a degree in sociology but no one will hire me." Unfortunately, there is not always a clear path between the educational system and the work world. Each has its own classification system designed for its own purposes.

A college major is usually housed under a broad academic discipline like communications, education, or business. Business, for example, is not just made up of one job but comprises many different specialty areas including accounting, actuarial science, economics, finance, information systems, international business, logistics, management, human resources, sales, real estate, and marketing. All these areas, or majors, relate to specific functions in the business world, and majoring in one area allows you to study those specific areas in-depth.

Sometimes majors are directly related to jobs in the workforce, and sometimes they're not. Accounting is considered a professional major because it prepares students for careers as professional accountants. Other majors, in particular the liberal arts majors like history, sociology, religious studies, communications, philosophy, etc., won't necessarily prepare you for one specific job but are designed to give students a set of skills that can be used in a variety of jobs. Communication, critical thinking, the ability to conduct research, and having an appreciation for other cultures are some of the skills these majors provide that may be used in the business world, at a nonprofit agency, in government, as a customer service supervisor, or in the admissions or registrar's office of a college or university.

HOW THE JOB MARKET IS ORGANIZED

In contrast with the college system of academic departments and majors, the job market is organized by industry and job function. Examples of *industries* are health care, finance, education, engineering, and manufacturing. Examples of *job functions* or *job families* are teaching, accounting, managing, and counseling. To get an idea of how the job market is organized, look at the classified section of any newspaper in the country. The following are some of the major job categories or industries that hire employees: *automotive, administration, clerical, customer service, education, general labor, health care, management, manufacturing, professional, retail, restaurant, sales, skilled, unskilled, and trade.*

If you read the job descriptions of the positions listed under each of these categories, you'll find each position requires a certain amount of training/ education, certification or licensing, skill in a particular area or with a certain piece of equipment, or a specified number of years of experience. In the work world, skills, experience, and education matter most to employers. Using the sociology example, you may have two degrees in sociology, but how do your degrees relate to the job market? Are you trained to perform a specific skill like accounting or nursing? Do you have any business or management experience with which to run a company or a bank? Are you certified to be a teacher? Our sociology graduate should be targeting jobs that require a college degree but do not specify any technical skills or certifications. Examples of these positions are sales, customer service, retail, or entry-level management positions.

IDENTIFYING YOUR SKILLS

Think about what you did in your first job, second job, and so on. Most of us are so busy *doing* our jobs that we don't have an opportunity to sit back and objectively look at what we do. Unless you have had practice in identifying your skills because you've prepared a resume or have recently gone through a job evaluation or appraisal, you are probably not used to viewing your job in this manner. Sometimes, it's helpful to look at old job descriptions or performance evaluations to get an idea of the main responsibilities of your job and the skills you use on a daily basis. Most people have more skills than they give themselves credit for.

One method that works well is the diary method: write down everything you did today from the time you went into work until you left at the end of the day. Do this for at least a week because you may do different aspects of your position during the work week. Then pick out the common job-related skills or responsibilities and summarize them.

Example:

> 8:00 am, said hello to Mrs. Smith as she came in the office and told Doctor Olson she was here for her appointment. Then pulled her chart and gave it to doctor's nurse.

If you do this repeatedly throughout the day, summarize this particular duty as "greeted and checked-in clients." A more sophisticated way to summarize these tasks would be to write "front-desk customer service."

I once worked with a woman who was the producer at a small radio station who wanted to find a different job in a related line of work. She was having trouble identifying her skills, so I asked her to summarize what she did at her job. She half-jokingly replied, "I guess not much of anything." I knew this wasn't true, so I gave her a homework assignment of making a list of everything she did at work at the end of each day. When she came in the following week, she had several pages of "stuff" written down. After summarizing common job responsibilities and organizing them by job category, she looked at me and said, "Wow, I actually *do* have skills!"

THE ART OF PUTTING YOUR SKILLS IN RESUME FORMAT

Work-related skills, including transferable skills, are typically best described with action verbs that say what you do, such as *teach, organize, design,* and *train.* Action verbs help to concisely and accurately describe the action being performed and give the job duty a more polished or professional sound.

When used in a resume or cover letter, the action verb is usually followed by the object (job task) of that verb, which is usually a noun (e.g., "children," "an awards ceremony," "a sales flyer," or "wait staff"). By connecting these together in the proper format, you would have the following descriptive sentences: "Taught at-risk children," "Organized an awards ceremony," "Designed a flyer," "Researched legal documents," and "Trained wait staff."

To create a concise, yet complete, descriptive sentence for a resume or cover letter, you should include enough information to answer the basic questions of *what* you did, *how* you did it, and what the *results* or *outcomes* were. Then write that description in an objective, past tense style. The previous examples would be written as, "Taught at-risk preschool children at two inner-city daycare centers," "Organized the annual United Way awards ceremony," and "Designed a promotional sales flyer that increased sales by 14%."

If you have been out of the workforce for several years, remember to use modern terminology to describe your skills so as not to date yourself. The following is a list of action words commonly used in today's work settings, organized by work function.

Work-Related Skills

Helping People:	Advised, aided, assessed, assisted, cared, coached, consulted, contacted, diagnosed, encouraged, evaluated, explained, informed, mediated, mentored, motivated, negotiated, recruited, referred, rehabilitated, represented, resolved, responded, scheduled, selected, supported, trained, taught, treated.
Ideas and Information:	Addressed, analyzed, applied, arbitrated, authored, categorized, collaborated, concluded, developed, drafted, edited, identified, implemented, formulated, interpreted, influenced, moderated, motivated, negotiated, participated, persuaded, presented, prioritized, proposed, publicized, researched, translated, wrote.
Data and Research:	Adjusted, applied, audited, calculated, clarified, coded, conducted, collected, compared, compiled, concluded, decreased, documented, estimated, evaluated, examined, experimented, extrapolated, increased, interpreted, interviewed, investigated, reviewed, solved, summarized, synthesized.

(Continued)

Financial:	Administered, allocated, audited, balanced, budgeted, calculated, counted, forecasted, invested, examined, projected, predicted, transferred.
Creative Process:	Acted, authored, constructed, conceptualized, conducted, created, customized, designed, developed, drafted, directed, edited, fabricated, illustrated, imagined, innovated, invented, originated, performed, pioneered, prepared, produced, published, recorded, redesigned, shaped, visualized, wrote.
Management:	Accomplished, administered, assigned, attained, chaired, communicated, conducted, consolidated, coordinated, directed, established, evaluated, hired, implemented, increased, initiated, led, managed, negotiated, organized, persuaded, planned, prioritized, recognized, resolved, reviewed, scheduled, strengthened, supervised, trained.
Office or Clerical:	Approved, arranged, classified, compiled, completed coordinated, created, expanded, distributed, filed, generated, improved, organized, performed, planned, prepared, processed, recorded, reduced, routed, scheduled, streamlined, updated.
Machines or Technology:	Adjusted, aligned, assembled, automated, designed, built, calibrated, computed, conducted, configured, controlled, devised, drove, eliminated, engineered, enhanced, fabricated, handled, inspected, installed, invented, maintained, monitored, operated, overhauled, processed, programmed, received, reduced, remodeled, repaired, retrieved, serviced, setup, solved, tested, trained, trouble-shot, upgraded.
Sales:	Acquired, advertised, communicated, convinced, contacted, demonstrated, improved, increased, marketed, met quota, motivated, negotiated, networked, obtained, partnered, persuaded, presented, proposed, sold, spoke.
Teaching or Training:	Adapted, assessed, coached, communicated, coordinated, corrected, created, defined, demonstrated, developed, designed, diagnosed, enabled, encouraged, evaluated, explained, facilitated, guided, implemented, informed, instructed, monitored, motivated, observed, persuaded, planned, prepared, set goals, stimulated, targeted, taught, trained, wrote.

Personal Characteristics and Soft Skills

Personal characteristics contribute to your success or accomplishments on the job. Certain traits are more effective in some industries than others. Being "aggressive" is a highly desirable trait if you are in sales or marketing, but it is not very effective if you are in a teaching or counseling profession. Employers and career professionals emphasize the importance of "soft skills" and cite the frequent absence of them in today's employees. Soft skills are the intangible qualities that will ultimately make or break an employee's ability to be successful. Because a lack of soft skills is often difficult to detect during the brief contact an employer has with a potential employee, many companies administer personality tests or ask behavioral-based interview questions as a regular part of the selection process.

Exercise 1: Place a check mark by any soft skills you believe you possess.

___Accurate	___Independent	___Resourceful
___Aggressive	___Logical	___Respectful
___Ambitious	___Loyal	___Responsible
___Calm	___Mature	___Self-Confident
___Cooperative	___Organized	___Sensitive
___Creative	___Patient	___Sincere
___Efficient	___Pleasant	___Strong
___Flexible	___Practical	___Thorough
___Friendly	___Problem-Solver	___Tolerant
___Helpful	___Quiet	___Trustworthy
___Honest	___Reliable	___Verbal

Creating Your Employability Package

Now let's complete your employability package. In the following exercise, include all current and former work-related skills (e.g., customer service, management, conflict resolution) as well as technical skills (e.g. Microsoft Office, FoxPro, Java, RPG, radiography). Regarding accomplishments, think about the times when you improved efficiency, changed a procedure for the better, increased sales, saved the company money, solved a problem, created, designed, or developed something from the ground up, coordinated a large event, implemented a new procedure, exceeded goals, quotas, or expectations, or received a promotion, award, or recognition.

Exercise 2: Your employability package.

Education (e.g., certificate, college degree, graduate work, on-the-job training, apprenticeships):

_____

_____

Licenses or Certifications (e.g., CISCO, R.N., CPR, licensed surveyor):

_____

Current Job Title: _____

Major Job Duties: _____

Time Employed: _____(years)

Accomplishments, Awards, Promotions: _____

_____

Previous Job Title: _____

Major Job Duties: _____

Time Employed: _____(years)

Accomplishments, Awards, Promotions: _____

_____

_____

Previous Job Title: _____

Major Job Duties: _____

Time Employed: _____(years)

Accomplishments, Awards, Promotions: _____

_____

Previous Job Title: _____

Major Job Duties: _____

Time Employed: _____(years)

Accomplishments, Awards, Promotions: _____

_____

Top Five Soft Skills (e.g., detail oriented, responsible, organized, analytical, good with people, creative, patient, calm in a crisis, meets deadlines):

1. _____

2. _____

3. _____

4. _____

5. _____

Major Strengths or Areas of Expertise (summarize, in one or two sentences, what you are really good at, or what you can do well such as repairing air conditioners, dealing with difficult teens, programming languages, etc.):

1. _____

2. _____

3. _____

4. _____

5. _____

What do the results of the above exercise tell you? Are you satisfied with what you see? Is there a skill you would like to acquire, or an area of expertise you wish you had? (Incidentally, you now have an important section of your resume completed!)

Matching Your Skills to the Requirements of the Job

When applying for a job, compare the items you listed in your employability package with the requirements in a job opening. Begin by reviewing the job title and the job description of the position you wish to apply for. Both can give you clues as to what an employer is looking for. Some job titles sound more complicated or technical than they really are. These include "assistant," "coordinator," "aide," and "technician" (but not if paired with a technical qualifier like "engineering" or "automotive"). When reviewing a job description, ask yourself the following questions:

1. What can be inferred from the job title?
2. What is the educational level required for the position?
3. What are the job duties and responsibilities?

4. Are there any skills, years of experience, particular software programs, or specific work experience required for the position?

5. Is there any technical jargon or occupation-specific terminology used in the job description ("just-in-time purchasing," "Microsoft Office applications," "Quark Xpress")?

Now, read the job description. Look closely at the skills and experience required for the position. "Required" generally means you will not get the position unless you have those skills, but "preferred" means the employer would like the candidate to have those skills, but it doesn't mean they will rule you out if you don't possess those skills. If the position requires a bachelor's degree and you have an associate degree, then you can assume that you won't be selected for an interview unless there is some flexibility on the part of the employer. This is especially true in educational institutions. However, if the job description includes a caveat that says "or equivalent work experience," then go ahead and apply for the position.

Let's look at Barb, a woman in her early thirties, who is the mother of two small children. Barb has a high school diploma supplemented with a few basic computer courses. Her previous work experience consists of volunteering a few hours a week as a secretary for her church and working part time at a department store over the Christmas holidays. She recently organized the annual church bazaar, is a member of the PTA at the school where her children attend, and often volunteers at the local nursing home where her mother resides.

Because Barb's children are now in elementary school, she has decided to go back to work. The job she is applying for is a receptionist position in a multidoctor chiropractic office located about ten minutes from her home. The job description reads as follows: *Seeking a receptionist for a busy chiropractic office. Responsibilities include greeting clients upon arrival in a professional manner, scheduling appointments, answering a multiline phone, and forwarding calls as appropriate. This position also supports the office staff with light typing, filing, copying, and faxing.*

The key requirements (skills) are customer service and basic typing skills. Barb's transferable work-related skills that match this position are as follows:

1. Customer service experience from part-time work in the department store.

2. Familiarity with Microsoft Word from her previous computer classes and office experience from her church position.

3. Demonstrated ability to work with the public from her job at the department store and her volunteer work on the church bazaar.

4. Telephone skills from answering the phone at church.

5. Organizational skills from overseeing details of the church bazaar (recruiting volunteers, arranging for food and entertainment, overseeing the budget) and serving on various PTA committees at her children's school.

Because there is no educational requirement for this position, it appears that Barb's high school diploma and computer classes should be adequate for the position. A key soft skill of the position is "greeting clients in a professional manner." Furthermore, we can infer from the industry (medical office) and the type of job (customer service and administrative support) that the employer will be looking for someone with good people skills and professional office etiquette and who will work well with others in a team environment. Barb describes herself as friendly, patient, well organized, and has the ability to make people (especially children and the elderly) feel at ease. These traits and strengths should meet the soft skill requirements of this position.

In drawing upon Barb's transferable work skills from both her paid and volunteer work experience, it appears that Barb's skills, experience, and soft skills are a close match to those required in the position. Therefore, Barb should have a very good chance of successfully competing for, and getting, this position.

If Barb were applying for a position in a business office doing accounts payable/receivable, she would not be as well qualified and would need to acquire some experience in a business setting or take a few classes in accounting and business. If she wanted to apply for a secretarial position that required proficiency in Microsoft Office applications, she could brush up her skills on her own or take some classes in Word, Access, Excel, and PowerPoint through the continuing education department at her local community college.

Exercise 3.

Now it's your turn. Look at the job description of an advertised job opening in your field. Then complete the following exercise using the information found in the job description.

1. Type of Industry (health care, business, etc.): _____

2. Level of Responsibility (management, staff, clerical): _____

3. Job Title: _____

  4. Required Educational Level: _____

  5. Years of Experience: _____

  6. Required Skills: _____

  7. Credentials: _____

  8. Special Knowledge: _____

  9. Required Soft Skills: _____

Exercise 4.

Now review your personal, work-related, and nonwork-related skills and experience and compare your skills with the requirements of the position.

1. Do I have the educational level and credentials?
   What are they? _____
2. Do I have the required number of years of experience in the right areas?
   Number of years and areas _____
3. Do I possess the special skills or knowledge required?
   What are they? _____
4. Can I do the required job duties and responsibilities?
   What can I do? _____
5. Do I possess the required soft skills?
   What do I possess? _____
6. Why am I a good candidate for this position?
   Explain _____

The formula for successfully finding a job is really quite simple: The closer the match between your skills, education, and experience and what an employer in a particular industry is looking for, the better your chances are of finding employment.

These exercises should do two things: either (1) make you feel really good about yourself and boost your confidence regarding your ability to go out and find another job, or (2) dramatically reveal any gaps between what you possess and what is needed to qualify for a good job. Many people find that education is one of the glaring items missing from their list. What item do you still need to make you more marketable in the workforce or in your profession?

Chapter 5

Make a Career Decision

Though no one can go back and make a brand new start, my friend, anyone can start from now and make a brand new end.

Carl Bard

Career development is the process of discovering who you are and where you fit in the work world. It is a process that involves redefining your career interests and commitments over your lifetime depending on the circumstances and life experiences that occur along the way. No one can decide what the best career is for you; only you can make that determination. So take an active approach in the process and be aware of any external influences on your decision-making.

The terms *career*, *job*, and *occupation* are often used interchangeably, although they are actually quite different. A *career* is a series of work experiences, usually in the same area, that is pursued over a person's lifetime. A career encompasses more than income and benefits, it is a lifetime progression of using your skills, education, knowledge, and experiences. A *job* refers to a specific position within an occupation. A job sometimes implies a source of paid income, or what you do for a living, not necessarily who or what you are. An *occupation* is a category of jobs that are grouped together because of similar characteristics. It is generally referred to as someone's "vocation," "business," "calling," "profession," or "trade." Workers within a single occupation may have many different job titles. For example, the *teaching* occupation includes English teachers, special education teachers, health teachers, history teachers, and art teachers. Although a person could have several jobs within an occupation or among occupations, a career usually spans a period of time. Perception often plays a role in these definitions. What is considered a *career* for one person may be viewed as just a *job* to another. Law is considered a *career* within the larger grouping of legal *occupations*. But practicing law could also be considered just a *job* if you dread going to work each morning and view it only as a way to pay the bills until you are able to do what you really enjoy.

CAREER DECISION-MAKING 101

The career decision-making process involves six basic steps. In this chapter, we will primarily focus on the process of self-assessment, generating options, and making a decision (steps 1 through 4). Steps 5 and 6 will be discussed in Chapters 8 and 11.

Step 1: Start with who you are. Make a list of what you enjoy, what you're good at, and what's important in your life and in a career. Ask yourself these questions: What kinds of people would I like to work with? What kind of job settings would I most enjoy? What skills do I want to use on the job? What challenges and rewards do I enjoy? What types of work environments would make me happy? If you need help identifying possible occupations based on your interests, values, and personality, you may want to take an "interest inventory." Interest inventories can be obtained from the career center at your local college.

Step 2: Identify one to three career options that contain the things you enjoy, allow you to do what you're good at, and will help you obtain success and satisfaction in your life. Keep an open mind; don't discount careers because of their title or status. Be aware of biases based on incomplete or faulty information about careers (examples: teachers don't make very much money, retail jobs are all about folding sweaters at The Gap).

Step 3: Get the facts. Research the career options you identified. Because of popular television shows like *CSI*, many people want to pursue forensic science until they learn that a science degree is required. There are advantages and disadvantages to every career. The trick is to find one that best fits your strengths, personality, and work habits, and the only way to discover this is to do some serious research. Look on the Internet, ask your teachers, talk to neighbors or family members. If you're interested in becoming a physical therapist, for example, call your local rehab center and see whether there is someone who would be willing to spend a few minutes talking to you about his or her job.

Step 4: Make a decision. Once you've researched your options, weighed the pros and cons, discussed it with others, and narrowed down your options to one or two careers, you should be able to make a decision.

Choose a career that best matches your interests, skills, abilities, values, and personality style.

Step 5: Make a plan. Once you've made a career decision, you are ready to draft a plan of action. What will you need to do to reach your career goal? Will you need to go back to school? How much education will you need, and where will you obtain your education? How will you finance your education? What certifications or licensing requirements must you meet after you graduate?

Step 6: Just do it. Based on the information you have gathered and analyzed, you're ready to start taking classes or searching for a new job. Periodically review and reflect on your decision and your course of action. Make the needed adjustments to your career plans; people do this all the time. It's just part of the decision-making process.

STEP 1: SELF-ASSESSMENT

Many people come into my office and begin a conversation by saying, "I want a better job," or, "I hate my job because it's too boring," or "I need something that's more exciting," or, "I want a job that pays more." But when I ask them what they would like to do differently, or what would be more exciting, they have no idea. Although I understand where these individuals are coming from, they are reacting from an emotional level that, although temporarily therapeutic, doesn't get them any closer to finding the job they want. What is "interesting" and "exciting" to one person can be boring or draining to another. Someone who loves the English language and values accuracy and detail will find a job as a proofreader satisfying, whereas someone who values talking with many different types of people on a daily basis would find proofreading boring beyond comprehension.

Self-assessment is the process of exploring and identifying your interests, values, motivations, tendencies, and personality traits. The first step in self-assessment is being able to define what is "interesting" or "exciting" to you. This is a personal definition. Once you can articulate your interests, values, personality style, passions, and motivators, then you can begin to identify occupations that contain those elements. This is why most career counseling approaches begin by asking you to identify your interests. Doing a job that you truly enjoy is going to make you happier in the long run.

Begin the self-assessment process by setting aside a few hours a day to resurrect your dreams and listen to your inner voice. Make a list of what you enjoy doing, feel passionate about, or consider your calling. Try to construct this list without thinking about the pressures and concerns in your daily life.

Focusing too much on current concerns inhibits the creative process. Just brainstorm. There will be plenty of time for reality testing.

The following exercises are designed to help you get in touch with your interests and passions.

Exercise 1: Daydreams

Answer the following questions by filling in the blank.

1. The hours seem to fly by when _____
2. I often lose track of time when _____
3. I am happiest when _____
4. I wish I could _____ all day long
5. If I had a zillion dollars, I would _____

Exercise 2: Back to the past

If you are having difficulty identifying what you enjoy, sometimes going back to the past will help identify life themes, influencing factors, and forgotten interests. Answer the following questions:

1. When you were a child, what did you want to be when you grew up? Why?
2. What subjects did you enjoy in high school? In which subjects did you receive your highest grades?
3. What did you do in your spare time? After school? On the weekends? What were your hobbies?
4. What were you good at? Did you earn any awards, a letter in track, or win a contest?
5. Did you have any special talents (art, music, sports)? Are you still pursuing these activities? Why or why not?
6. What extracurricular activities did you participate in during high school?
7. What did your parents/guardians do for a living? Your grandparents? Aunts and uncles? Other close relatives? How did this influence you?
8. What are your strongest personal qualities? How would someone describe you? What do your friends like the most about you?

It is worthwhile to reflect on your past to discover the core interests you had as a child, before life got in the way. Can you identify any major influences or trends? If you did not attend college, what were the circumstances behind that decision? Why didn't you become the teacher you always wanted to be? Have any of those factors changed today? Do those reasons still exist? Do the same obstacles or priorities that prevented you from pursuing your dreams still exist today?

Think about what the events are that are causing you to consider making a change at this point in your life. Look at both the good and the not so good things that have happened over the course of your life. Is there anything you can learn from those events? Is there anything that you can use now to move your life forward?

Most of us tend to focus on what went wrong, and although we can all certainly learn from our mistakes, let's turn it around and look at what went right. What were the circumstances behind what went well? Can you use those skills, knowledge, strategies, or events to move forward now? Take this time to think deeply about what you want out of life. Do you have any unused talents that you'd like to develop? Perhaps there is a former hobby that can be catapulted into a part-time or full-time job.

Exercise 3: People, data, and things

Another simple, but very effective, exercise is to identify which you would prefer working with on a daily basis: People, Data, or Things. The People, Data, and Things taxonomy formed the core of the "Functional Job Analysis" theory developed by Sidney Fine in 1955 and was later incorporated into the job classification system used by the *Dictionary of Occupational Titles*. The People, Data, and Things system essentially states that all work activity can be described in terms of the level of its involvement with People, Data, and Things.[1]

The **People** category involves working with people and animals. Job tasks include advising, coaching, helping, influencing, interviewing, managing, mentoring, motivating, negotiating, public speaking, selling, supervising, persuading, teaching, training, and tutoring.

Possible careers:

- Education
- Counseling, psychology, or social work
- Medical or health care
- Fitness and nutrition
- Personal services
- Sales

- Customer service
- Management
- Legal services
- Entertainment
- Politics
- Veterinary science
- Animal care or training

Data and Information consist of working with facts, numbers, words, symbols, ideas, concepts, and business procedures. Job tasks include accounting, analyzing, balancing, budgeting, collecting, compiling, computing, creating, designing, estimating, evaluating, forecasting, imagining, inputting, organizing, planning, problem solving, surveying, sorting, synthesizing, and transcribing.
Possible careers:

- Computer science and programming
- Economics
- Engineering
- Finance and banking
- Mathematics
- Record keeping
- Office procedures
- Research
- Writing

Things are substances or materials, machines, tools, equipment, work aids, and products. Job tasks include assembling, calibrating, constructing, cooking, crafting, growing, packaging, inspecting, maintaining, manufacturing, operating, planting, preparing, repairing, and setting up.
Possible careers:

- Architecture
- Art
- Carpentry
- Culinary
- Construction
- Interior or fashion design

- Electronics
- Forestry
- Horticulture
- Landscape design or construction
- Maintenance and repair
- Music
- Photography
- Production work
- Trucking

Interest Inventories

If you are very confused or undecided about your future career, you may want to take an interest inventory. Sometimes, interest inventories are also called career tests, but they are not really *tests* because there are no right or wrong answers. Interest inventories are designed to help identify possible career options based on your likes and dislikes. Many are based on the work of John Holland, a noted career theorist. According to John Holland, most people and most occupations can be categorized into six basic personality types and job characteristics. By their inherent nature, certain personality types are better suited to certain occupations. Someone who is very detailed oriented and reacts to change in a slow, thoughtful manner is not going to do well in a work environment characterized by chaos and unpredictability. Likewise, some-one who enjoys being around people and thrives on interpersonal interactions is not going to be as happy in an isolated work situation where there is little daily contact with people. Ability and motivation aside, these factors will make the difference between being satisfied in your job or being miserable.

The Self-Directed Search (SDS) was developed by John Holland and is a quick, reliable tool that can be taken in a pencil-and-paper format or online at www.sds.com for a minimal fee. Other popular standardized interest inventories are the *Campbell Interest and Skill Survey*, the *Strong Interest Inventory*, and the *Jackson Vocational Interest Survey*. Another popular instrument is the *Myers-Briggs Type Inventory* (MBTI). The MBTI is not an interest inventory. It is based on Carl Jung's theory of psychological types and indicates a person's preference for gathering information and making decisions. The results can then be used to help people find work that is meaningful and at which they can be productive. The MBTI is surprisingly insightful and accurate in helping people identify career options, especially when combined with the results of an interest inventory.

Although any of these inventories can be taken online, you will get the most out of the information if you discuss the results with someone who is experienced in interpreting interest inventories. Make an appointment with a career counselor or life coach or contact the career services office of your local college or university. Some colleges charge a small fee for the general public to use their services, whereas many do not.

Abilities, Talents, Strengths, and Weaknesses

Knowing your strengths and weaknesses is critical to being successful in your profession. Just as a good coach puts his or her players in positions they can be most successful at and score the most points, so you will want to put yourself in a position where you are going to succeed.

Most people enjoy doing what they do well. However, sometimes our interests are not aligned with our strengths. You need to be objective about your abilities and fully comprehend the requirements of the occupation you want to pursue. However, that doesn't mean you have to eliminate that passion from your life. If you love dancing, for example, but do not have what it takes to successfully perform at a professional level, you can still incorporate dance in your life by performing on an amateur level, teaching dance, attending dance performances, or joining a civic organization that promotes dance in your community. Many people, especially artists, make the decision to work at one job during the day just to pay the bills and then pursue what they really love on the weekends. Most of us have multiple interests, talents, and hobbies. Being involved in a variety of activities is what keeps us balanced and happy and makes our lives full and rewarding.

Sometimes, people think there is only one "right" career. The reality is that most of us can be happy and satisfied in a number of careers or jobs. If you really want to be a nurse, ask yourself if it is because you want to work in a hospital environment, love medicine, or want to care for ill people? If your answer is that it will allow you to take care of people, then you may be just as happy working as a physician's assistant, a physical therapist, a social worker, a home health aide, on a hospital admissions staff, as an x-ray tech, or as a director of a women's shelter.

Luckily, most career fields have similar or related jobs that can be just as satisfying and rewarding. If you can't be a neurosurgeon but still enjoy medicine and helping others, for example, there are plenty of other related health care careers such as nursing, radiology, physical or occupational therapy, speech pathology, physician assistant, or medical technology. Or you could become a medical counselor, social worker, genetic counselor, or other health professional that works with or for the neurosurgeon.

The key is to be able to identify those particular aspects of a profession that interest you. Once you've identified those key factors, you will find that there are several possible occupations that contain those key elements. Now, you've not only broadened your career options but have also avoided the common pitfall of being locked into only one career choice.

This is why self-assessment is so important. If you know what your strengths, weaknesses, interests, motivations, and passions are, you can make an appropriate occupational match. Just as people are made up of more than one attribute, so are occupations. A good occupational match is made when the essential factors that make up an individual match, or are at least compatible with, the dominant attributes of a job or career.

Work and Life Values

Values play an important role in the career planning process. If your values are expressed in your work, then your job or occupation takes on meaning and purpose. If your work does not provide personal satisfaction, then it becomes flat, meaningless, and boring. This is the source of dissatisfaction that causes many people to suddenly leave a highly successful career and pursue something else. Money, although helpful, does not guarantee happiness. If it did, all wealthy people would be completely satisfied with their lives.

People choose the careers they do for a variety of reasons. Some people pursue an occupation because they enjoy the wealth, power, and prestige that come with that occupation. Since the 1990s, there has been a trend toward creating lifestyles that have more meaning and make a contribution to the world. Others decide to choose a job that has less stress to gain personal happiness. Depending on your perspective or on your personal definition of happiness or success, this decision may also mean earning less pay or acquiring less prestige. If you enjoy medicine, for example, but don't want to spend the time or money to attend medical school or bear the cost of malpractice insurance or the responsibility that goes along with practicing medicine, you might opt for a career as a physician assistant or a respiratory therapist. These alternative professions will still allow you to pursue your love of medicine and desire to help people and earn a decent salary. The added bonus is that you just might discover that your work is just as fulfilling, without all the stress and responsibility of being a physician.

For most people, values change or deepen as they grow older and go through more life experiences. Some of the motivation behind a career changer's visit to my office may stem from the larger life issue of trying to create a more fulfilling or meaningful life. A new career can mean a fresh start or a better life (whatever that is to you).

Some of you may decide to pursue a particular career based on salary because you are underemployed or a single parent who is trying to provide a better lifestyle for your family. This is an admirable value. However, ideally, you would want to choose a career that not only provided you with a sustainable income but one that you enjoyed doing.

Employers are generally more interested in your abilities than your values because they want people who can produce results for their company or organization. You, however, may be more motivated from the personal satisfaction you receive from a job. Being able to identify and prioritize your work values will help you make a better choice of work environments and increase the likelihood that you will find a career that makes getting up in the morning to go to work a pleasure.

Exercise 4: Values

Circle the values that are important to you:

Achievement	Love
Accuracy	Loyalty
Advancement	Morality/ethics
Autonomy	Order
Beauty	Public contact
Challenge	Quality
Competition	Recognition
Cooperation	Relationships
Creativity	Reliability
Decision-making	Religious faith
Excitement	Respect
Family	Responsibility
Flexibility	Salary
Fun	Security
Helping others	Skill
Health/wellness	Solving problems
Honesty	Status and prestige
Independence	Solitude
Justice	Taking risks
Knowledge	Time to reflect or refuel
Managing others	Travel
Power and influence	Variety
Physical appearance	Wisdom
Physical challenge	Working as part of a team

Some values are more closely associated with a particular occupation than others. An occupation that allows you to be attractive and well liked, like modeling or acting, would be suitable for someone who valued physical appearance and recognition. Justice and social consciousness might be important values to someone in the legal profession, whereas altruism and emotional well-being would be important values for someone in a social work or counseling profession. Use your value system to help you select occupations that will provide you with the most meaning and fulfillment.

STEP 2: IDENTIFY CAREER POSSIBILITIES

I find it helpful to begin with a broad career area of interest and then narrow down the choices to one or two specific areas. Examples of broad career areas include agriculture, animals, art, business, communications, counseling or psychology, education, engineering, computer or information sciences, health care, health and wellness, mathematics, the liberal arts (humanities and social sciences), science, technology, and the skilled trades.

Our federal government uses the Standard Occupational Classification (SOC) system to organize all of the occupations that currently exist into several broad "categories." These categories are:

- Management
- Business and financial
- Computer and mathematical
- Architecture and engineering
- Life, physical, and social sciences
- Community and social services
- Legal
- Education, training, and library
- Arts, design, entertainment, sports, and media
- Health care practice
- Health care support
- Protective services
- Food preparation and serving
- Building, grounds cleaning, and maintenance
- Personal care and service

- Sales
- Office and administrative
- Farming, fishing, and forestry
- Construction and extraction
- Installation, maintenance, and repair
- Production, transportation, and material moving
- Military occupations

Exercise 5: Generating career alternatives

To help you identify career options, try using a variation on a career exploration exercise called "Everyone Can't Be a Superstar":

1. Behind every television star there is a make-up artist, stunt person, wardrobe consultant, agent, hairdresser, photographer, manager, writer, personal assistant, publicity director, accountant, and caterer.
2. Every rock star needs a recording technician, piano tuner, recording producer, sound editor, songwriter, concert coordinator, lighting director, costume designer, and choreographer.
3. Every person who sees a surgeon also needs the services of an anesthetist, nurse, surgical technologist, x-ray technician, physical therapist, speech pathologist, occupational therapist, social worker, admissions clerk, insurance coder, medical records director, dietician, and hospital administrator.

Think about a famous or prominent career or professional (e.g., a forensic scientist, professional athlete, movie director, publisher, architect, politician, defense lawyer, CEO of a company) and try to research all of the related, yet essential, positions that support that career or make it possible for that professional to be successful.

After you have selected one or two broad career areas that you definitely are interested in, try to narrow your choices down even further by selecting several occupations within those broad career categories. If you know that you would like to do something in the health care area, for example, research all of the careers that fall within that occupational category (medicine, dentistry, chiropractic, nursing, nutrition, physical therapy, occupational therapy, respiratory therapy, speech and language pathology, radiology, surgical technology, pharmacy, emergency medical services, and medical laboratory technology, etc.).

STEP 3: RESEARCH MAJORS OR CAREERS

Occupational research is critical to good career decision-making because your decision is only as good as the information you base it on. One of the main reasons people end up in a career they don't like is because they thought it was going to be something other than what it turned out to be.

Most people are aware of only a handful of available careers through the people they come into contact with on a daily basis. There are hundreds of occupations to choose from, and new ones are being developed every year. The *O*NET Dictionary of Occupational Titles* (online.onetcenter.org/) describes over 1,200 occupations that cover almost 100% of the jobs currently in the workplace. Once you've narrowed your search down to a few occupations, you're ready to use the *Occupational Outlook Handbook* (www. bls.gov/OCO/) to research each career more thoroughly. Before you can make a realistic decision about your career, it's important to take an informed look at all of the possibilities.

Exercise 6: Researching a career

Use the following questions as a guide when researching an occupation or career:

1. Description. What exactly does a person in this career do on a daily basis? Does this career require you to work primarily with people, data, ideas, or machines?

2. Work hours. Are the work hours during the daytime, evening, swing shift, 40 hours a week, or longer? Will you be expected to work overtime?

3. Work environment. Will you be working in an office environment, on the road, in a plant, in a hospital or clinic, or outdoors? Will you be part of a team or expected to work independently? How much autonomy or decision-making ability will you have? Is this a faster-paced or slower-paced work environment? What is the stress level in this job?

4. Salary and benefits. What is the starting wage or salary? Is the pay based on an hourly rate, annual salary, or commission? Are you paid weekly, monthly, or bimonthly? Are there opportunities for bonuses, raises, or advancement? What do you need to do to be successful in this career?

5. Credentials. What are the minimal requirements to enter this profession? What educational degree, training, certification, licensing, or

skills are required to enter this profession? Are there any special personal attributes, mental capacities, or physical requirements needed to perform the job tasks in this career?

6. What are the positive and negative aspects of this career?

7. Occupational outlook. What is the future job outlook for this career? Will there be a demand for this occupation five or ten years from now, or is the industry subject to economic fluctuations or local labor market demand?

There are many sources of career information. There are books written on every career imaginable located in the public library, at career centers at colleges and universities, or on the shelves of your favorite bookstore. The Internet is also a great source that provides current information from sources all around the world on a 24-7 basis. There are hundreds of good websites authored by professional organizations designed to educate people and promote their respective profession. The *Occupational Outlook Handbook* can be accessed online at http://online.onetcenter.org or http://www.bls.gov/OCO and contains detailed descriptions of hundreds of occupations.

An easy way to find information about careers is to use your Internet browser (*Google, Yahoo,* etc.). Simply type "Careers in (accounting, automotive, animals, fashion design, etc.)" in the search box to access a wealth of career-related websites. If you don't want to spend time wading through hundreds of websites, there are sites that have career information organized by occupation and industry. One example is America's Career InfoNet, which can be found at www.acinet.org. In addition, most states have websites about career opportunities in their geographic area, and most colleges and universities have links to career-related information on their career services websites. A more complete list of career-related websites is located in Appendix B.

Exercise 7: Informational interviewing

Talking with people about their jobs is an excellent way to get an insider's view of a job or career field. Here are some questions you may want to ask:

- What made you decide to choose this career?
- What was your career path?
- What are your responsibilities or job duties?
- What do you like and what do you dislike about this occupation?
- What is a typical day like on your job?

- What types of people, clients, patients, customers, coworkers, or other professionals do you interact with on a daily basis?
- What is the average starting salary for this job?
- What are the educational requirements of this job?
- What does it take to be successful in this career?
- Do you have any advice for someone considering this career?

Professional organizations are another good source of information about careers. Most careers are affiliated with a professional organization or accrediting body that maintains the educational and professional standards for the profession. Most of this information is available online and can provide you with detailed information about the profession, as well as career opportunities, educational requirements, professional activities, and a wealth of other information related to that profession. Most national organizations also have state, local, and student chapters. Contacting your state or local chapter may provide you with additional information or connect you with a professional in your area.

When you begin researching careers, compare the results of your self-assessment with the job description. Is there a match between your interests and work values and the characteristics of the job? How close or how distant is the match, and how willing are you to put up with the differences? Ask yourself whether this job will allow you to fully use your abilities, maintain your interest, feel fulfilled, not compromise your ideals, allow you to reach your goals, and live the type of life you have always dreamed about.

Exercise 8: Some final questions

When making a final career decision, ask yourself these questions:

1. Can I see myself doing this job all day long? For several years?
2. Do I have the ability to earn the degree or successfully complete the training that's required for this career?
3. Am I willing to spend the time necessary to complete my degree, training, or certification? Am I motivated enough to complete the program without stopping?
4. Do I have (or can I obtain) the financial resources needed to complete the requirements needed to enter this profession?
5. Why do I think I will be successful in this career or profession?

6. Will the work hours and conditions suit me? How well does this work environment match my personality style? How happy or unhappy will I be under these work conditions? Will this environment allow me to grow personally and professionally?

STEP 4: MAKE A DECISION

We make decisions every day. What to wear, what to order for lunch, what movie to see, what car or house to buy, etc. Think about how you make decisions. Do you ask others for advice or go by your gut feeling? Let's use buying a car as an example. How did you go about deciding which car to buy? Did you select a Toyota because your family has always bought Toyotas? Or because your friend, neighbor, or coworker recommended a Toyota? Did you ask your friends or relatives for their advice, or did you just let your spouse pick the car? Perhaps you researched the Camry on the Internet so when you went to the dealership, you already knew about the price, gas mileage, features, and options. When you visited the dealership, did you look at all of the cars and test drive a few before making a decision? Or did the salesperson's description influence your decision? What criteria did you use to make a selection? Was it the style, color, options, gas mileage, or safety features? Or perhaps it was how you looked in the car that made the decision for you? Perhaps your decision was based on your value system (made in America, environmentally responsible, safety features)?

There are three main decision-making styles: (1) *Rational*, decisions are made in a logical and intentional fashion, (2) *Intuitive*, decisions are based on feelings and emotional responses, and (3) *Dependent*, decisions are based on others' opinions.[2] To some extent, we may use information from all three decision-making styles, depending on our needs and purposes, although one style is usually prevalent in the majority of situations.

When it comes to making a decision about a career, it is helpful to have already identified the criteria you will be basing your decision on. In other words, know what you like to do at work and why, how your value system influences where you work, what makes you feel rewarded or satisfied, the amount of pay you desire, the location of the job, the physical work environment, and the culture or type of people you want to work in or with.

I would encourage you to adopt a fact-based decision-making process. After you have done your research and weighed all the evidence, then you will be ready to make a decision. Use your intuition and your feelings to help you identify initial areas of interest or what office environments or employers feel "right" to you but then use a fact-based process to make the best decision for yourself and your situation.

Carefully evaluate the costs, risks, and both the positive and negative aspects of each occupation. Many people make poor career choices because they really didn't understand what they were getting into. You can minimize the chance of making a "bad" choice by doing your homework ahead of time. Other people allow family members or situations to dictate their decisions rather than making decisions themselves. Making a decision based on what you want to do and what is best for your particular situation will not only give you a sense of empowerment, it will result in more career satisfaction in the long run. There is no shortage of opinions in the world. Anyone can tell you what to do, but you will be the one doing that job for eight hours each day, not them.

Exercise 9: Choosing a career questionnaire

Complete the following questionnaire using the results of the previous exercises.

Choosing a Career Questionnaire

1. Which would you prefer to work with? (circle one)
   People   Data   Things

2. Interests? (please list)   Hobbies?

   _____   _____
   _____   _____
   _____   _____
   _____   _____

3. What are you good at? (your abilities/skills/training/knowledge)

   _____   _____
   _____   _____
   _____   _____

4. Personality (describe yourself using adjectives)

   _____   _____
   _____   _____
   _____   _____

5. Wishes (what would you do if you could?)
   _____
   _____
   _____

(*continued*)

6. Rate your work values (on a scale of 1–5 based on importance)

Amount of supervision? ___   Helping others? ___
Amount of pressure? ___   Solving problems?___
Amount of variety? ___   Being creative? ___
Amount of time with the public? ___ Time alone? ___
Salary? ___   Status/prestige? ___
Directing others? ___   Seeing the results? ___
Being part of a team? ___   Competition? ___

7. Based on your answers to questions 1–6, these are your possible career areas:
a. _____
b. _____
c. _____

PUTTING IT ALL TOGETHER

Let's end with a couple of case studies to show how to move forward to a new career.

Jeff is thirty-six years old, married, and the father of two children. His wife works as a medical secretary at a local chiropractic clinic. Jeff has been a salesman for a large manufacturing company for the past six years but is getting tired of a commissioned position that does not offer enough job stability. Lately, he seems to be traveling more because his new regional manager is focused on expanding their territory. All the traveling makes it difficult to spend time with his boys and attend their after-school sports activities.

Jeff has a bachelor's degree in communications and a strong interest in computers. He also plays bass guitar in a local band on the weekends. Results of the *Strong Interest Inventory* reveal a SEC (Social, Enterprising, and Conventional) code. Possible career areas include teaching, entrepreneurship, data information, and computer programming.

Because Jeff has always wanted to be a teacher, he has begun looking into the possibility of becoming a high school math teacher. Teaching really appeals to Jeff because of the steady income and the stability of belonging to a union. In addition, teaching meets Jeff's values of having summers and holidays off to spend with his sons. Because of the demand for math teachers in his state, Jeff learned that a math teacher's salary would pay about $15,000 to $20,000 more than he is currently making.

After meeting with the dean of education at his local university, Jeff discovered that because he already has a bachelor's degree, he would only need to complete the required courses necessary for teacher certification, about thirty credits. This is a big relief to both Jeff and his wife, who wondered how they would continue to pay the bills while Jeff returned to school. To keep a source of income, Jeff has decided to continue working at his job while completing as many courses as possible at night. When the time comes to do his student teaching, he will apply for financial aid, quit his job, and enroll full time to complete the remaining courses.

Regina has been working in the office of an electronics manufacturing plant that recently shut down because of increased global competition. Regina is thirty-four, single, and qualifies for Trade Act Assistance (TAA) benefits, which will allow her to go back to school for two years while retaining her unemployment benefits. After talking with Regina about what she'd like to pursue, she indicated that she is tired of sitting at a computer all day. Instead, she would prefer to work in an environment where she can move around and still help people. Her Holland Code is RAS (Realistic, Artistic, Social). Her hobbies include coaching the local girls' basketball team, spending time outdoors, hiking, skiing, and rock climbing.

Regina was initially considering criminal justice or environmental science. After researching these careers, she decided that she is really not interested in security work, which is where many of the criminal justice positions are in her area. Even though she enjoys working outside and is environmentally conscious, she is not sure she has the resources or motivation to pursue a four-year degree in environmental science. During her occupational research, Regina came across the paramedic profession. The fast pace and physical aspect of being a paramedic appeals to Regina. In addition, she thinks she can utilize her attention to detail to assess the emergency scene and her coaching skills to help patients remain calm while first aid is administered. Regina's local community college offers a two-year paramedic program, which would give her more advanced training than an EMT degree. Because that program qualifies for TAA benefits, she has decided to enroll the next semester.

Chapter 6

Identify Your Options

If you always do what you've always done, you will always get what you always got.
Anonymous

Each of you, regardless of your unique employment situation, has a number of options to choose from. The following options are listed for each type of job seeker. Find the category that best describes your situation and consider the options offered. Each option will be discussed in more detail throughout this chapter.

Situation A: Recently Unemployed Because of a Layoff

- Find another job similar to your former position or profession.
- Go back to school and train for a new career.
- Start your own business.
- Take an early retirement.

Situation B: Forced to Find a New Career Because of Injury

- Remain in your profession but work in a different capacity.
- Find a different job with your current employer.
- Find a different job with a new employer.
- Go back to school to upgrade skills or train for a new career.
- Start your own business.
- Continue on long-term disability or take an early retirement.

Situation C: Reentering the Workforce after an Absence

- Resume your previous job.
- Find a different job with your previous employer.
- Find a job with a new employer.
- Go back to school to upgrade skills or train for a new career.
- Start your own business.

Situation D: Employed but Looking for a Different Job

- Stay where you are.
- Transfer to a different job within your current organization or company.
- Find a similar job with a different employer.
- Start your own business.
- Go back to school to upgrade your skills or train for a new career.
- Take an early retirement.

SAME EMPLOYER, NEW JOB

If you like your boss or the company you work for but are bored or dissatisfied with your job, then it's worth investigating whether there is anything you can change about your current situation to make it more tolerable, like moving to a different department or assuming a new set of duties and responsibilities. If you are in customer service, for example, and are burned out from the constant phone interaction with unhappy customers, is it possible to move to the bookkeeping department or some other area of the company that doesn't require as much phone work or customer contact? Or, if you have been working in an office setting that requires too much solitary time on the computer and you need more interaction with people, is it possible to move to the reception or customer service areas within your company? Sometimes, just moving to a new department with fresh faces and a new set of responsibilities is enough to give you a fresh perspective and a renewed sense of purpose.

Moving to a new department or position is easier to accomplish in a large organization where there is more room to move around. Moving to a new area also assumes that you have the required skills to do the job in that department. If you think you'd like to move to a different position but know that you currently lack keyboarding skills or familiarity with a particular database or accounting package, then you may want to begin planning for the move by brushing up your skills with a few classes at night. Because you are still employed, you will have the time to prepare and position yourself for an opening in that department when it becomes available.

If you need to change positions because of injury, illness, or disability, talk with your employer or human resources department about the possibility of assuming another position that would allow you to remain employed and productive but not aggravate your injuries. For example, if you hurt your back and can no longer unload boxes in the warehouse, is it possible to move into another position in the plant that doesn't require lifting?

SAME JOB, DIFFERENT EMPLOYER

If you still enjoy the actual work you do at your job, but not who you're working for, then this option may be for you. Many people leave jobs because they dislike the people they work with more than they dislike the job duties. Before you quit your job, try to see whether you can improve your situation by talking to those involved or changing your approach to those who irritate you. If you have tried everything you can to improve your work environment, even to the point of trying to move to a different department with another supervisor, then the only remaining choice is to leave. Many companies lose good employees this way, but the loss is their loss and your gain.

The benefits of moving to another employer are a fresh start in a new atmosphere with an employer who will recognize and appreciate your talents. This option allows you to retain your professional skills, discard the emotional baggage of your old position, and recharge your enthusiasm and passion for work. In my personal experience, it is sometimes the only option that allows employees to move into higher levels or better-paying positions that may not have ever been possible at their previous place of employment. Just like actors/actresses who find themselves typecast into one role, so can employees who work at one position for a long time end up being stereotyped. "Once a secretary, always a secretary" is often the mantra. That's why it's so difficult for a secretary to move into a managerial position, because everyone else in the organization still views that person as just a "secretary."

If you were previously in a professional field, and you've kept your credentials and your skills up to date, great! If not, find out from your professional organization or licensing board what you will need to do to renew your license or certification. Science and health care professions change quickly, and your certification (and your skills) may be out of date if it has been five or more years since you've worked in your field.

If you were, or are about to be, laid off, ask your former supervisor to provide a letter of reference or assistance finding a new position. Many companies now offer outplacement services. Use any former contacts, clients, or professional associates to help you search for job openings.

RELATED JOB, DIFFERENT EMPLOYER

This option allows you to retain your past experience and skills but applies them in a slightly different direction. A nurse who is feeling burned out after working twenty years in the emergency room may be able to rekindle her passion for her profession in a fresh setting. By applying her clinical skills and ability to remain calm during a crisis to a position in a pediatric ward, home health care facility, school district, or college setting, she can salvage all of her training and education while avoiding the original stressors that contributed to her burnout. If she wanted to take a step further and leave the hospital or clinical environment altogether, she could look for a position as a claims examiner with an insurance company or with Social Security Disability. With a little more education, she could even become a clinical instructor in a nursing program at her local college.

Your skills and level of education beyond high school will determine the ease or difficulty of transferring your work experience to a related field. In general, the more closely related a new career is to your existing position, the easier it is to transition into that career. You want to capitalize on your strengths, emphasize any past experiences that are related to your new profession, and update your credentials. A sales professional, for example, could easily transfer his or her skills to become a corporate trainer, a fund-raiser, public relations staff member, a customer service supervisor, or an admissions representative at a college. With the addition of a few business courses, he or she may be able to move into the marketing, advertising, or public relations fields.

Individuals who have science or math backgrounds and previous industry experience can enter education, sales, or city government, teach at colleges or universities, work as consultants to companies in related industries or nonprofit organizations, or find employment as editors or science consultants to book and trade magazine publishers.

Former public school teachers can become educational consultants, administrators, provide freelance tutoring or grant writing services, move into faculty, administrative, or student services positions at colleges and universities, or find employment in nonprofit agencies or educational sales. An English teacher tired of the public school environment may find renewed interest working as an editor for a magazine, newspaper, or a book publishing company. The opportunities are endless if you just use a little imagination.

DIFFERENT JOB, NEW EMPLOYER

Many people choose to make a 360-degree change and look for a brand-new career field. This option is appropriate for someone who no longer enjoys their profession and needs something new.

If you have been laid off or downsized and have been unsuccessfully searching for work for over a year, you may want to consider a new career field. If you have been searching for work on a regular basis but haven't received any invitations to interview for several months, one of two things may have happened: (1) you are no longer marketable in your industry or (2) the industry is tapped out of opportunities. In either case, it may be time to change to a different line of work.

Making a radical career change will invariably require going back to school. Many occupations require special credentials or a prescribed level of educational attainment. If you are a production worker with no education beyond high school who wants to become a registered nurse, you will need to go back to school to earn a nursing degree and then pass a state licensing examination. However, there are a few exceptions. If you already have a bachelor's degree and possess good communication skills and computer literacy, you could transition into manufacturing or retail sales or customer service, become an insurance agent, financial services consultant, or financial planner, go into entry-level human resources or public relations, or become a management trainee in almost any nontechnical industry.

Today, many colleges offer programs on an accelerated basis or by distance education, which may make the idea of going back to school to earn a new degree more palatable. If you already know what you would like to change your career to, you can begin researching colleges in your area that offer that program. If you are unsure of what you want to do in the future, you may want to enlist the help of a career or vocational counselor or a career coach to help you identify your areas of interest and some possible career options. Those professionals, including admissions and career services personnel at colleges and universities, can also provide information about specific occupations, job outlook, salary, and possible employers.

Making a career change at this point in your life will involve some sacrifice. You must carefully research your options and determine whether leaving your career or job is the best decision for you at this time. Determine whether what you will gain is worth the time or money you will sacrifice. Don't forget to factor into your decision the transferability of retirement benefits and the loss of any accumulated sick, personal, or vacation days.

GOING BACK TO SCHOOL

If you are thinking about moving to a better-paying position within your organization, going back to school to earn a degree or certification will give you a competitive edge. If you've been looking for a job in your field for longer than a year and have exhausted all other possibilities and resources (including the services of a professional recruiter), it may be time to switch gears and head in a new direction. In general, you want to work up, not down, by earning an advanced degree. Remember that two associate degrees do not equal a bachelor's degree any more than do two bachelor's degrees equal a master's degree. So, if you already have an associate degree or certificate, consider earning a bachelor's degree. If you already have a bachelor's degree, consider graduate courses, a graduate degree, or a marketable professional certification.

Examples of jobs that require little skill upgrade (less than one year) are dental assisting, LPN certification, and Microsoft Office certification. Occupations that require at least two years of school (associate degrees) are nursing, HVAC, veterinary technician, and computer information systems. Professions like education, engineering, and business will require a four-year (baccalaureate) degree, whereas other professional fields such as counseling, social work, library science, physical therapy, occupational therapy, and speech pathology require a master's degree. To become a physician, veterinarian, lawyer, optometrist, pharmacist, or dentist requires three to four years of enrollment in a professional program beyond a bachelor's degree.

In a few cases, it may be more profitable to add on a highly marketable associate degree or certificate to your bachelor's degree. This will depend on the marketplace and the value or demand of the technical skills you want to acquire. I have worked with several students who already held a bachelor's degree but then, for one reason or another, decided to come back to school and pick up another highly marketable two-year degree (like registered nursing, cyber security, or surveying technology). After passing their respective licensing examinations, they were able to make more money in their new career than they ever did with their former degrees. Again, it all depends on what's hot in the job market and where your interests lie.

For example, if you have been in human resources all your life but find that the job market in your area is stale, try taking some advanced courses and applying your previous experience to a related business field such as marketing, OSHA regulation enforcement, purchasing, health care policy administration, or consider teaching undergraduate or graduate level business courses at your local college or university.

If you have been laid off and are considering returning to school, you will want to find out whether your employer is offering any severance pay or outplacement services to help you finance your education or retrain for a new career. Visit your local One-Stop Career Center (old unemployment office) and inquire about any state or federal funding (e.g., TAA benefits) for individuals in your situation. One-Stop Career Centers are designed to help you with all of your employment and job training needs. Depending on which state or county you live in, they may be called an Employment Center, CareerLink, Workforce Center, Job Center, Works, or Employment and Training Center. The location of a center in your area can be found at www.CareerOneStop.org.

Other sources include your local Office of Vocational Rehabilitation to see whether you qualify for any retraining monies because of disability or making an appointment with the admissions office at your local college or university to inquire about any student aid assistance or scholarships they may offer.

STARTING YOUR OWN BUSINESS

Many people are choosing the freedom and flexibility to become their own boss and manage their own business. This option is especially appealing to people who have been suddenly laid off or downsized and are finding it difficult to secure another job at the same salary they previously earned. Do you have a long-time passion that can be turned into a profitable career? Can you adapt any of your existing skills, expertise, or experience and apply them to a new venture? If you enjoy flower design in your spare time, can you volunteer or work part time at a local nursery or florist to build up your skills or begin building a clientele list by offering to do floral arrangements for weddings?

Home businesses have become very popular. Dry cleaning pickup and delivery, tailoring, adventure tours, pet and house sitting, mobile massage, computer repair, eldercare, professional event planning, tutoring, art, music, or dance lessons, tax preparation, patent or title searching, cleaning services, temporary staffing services, and home repair services are just some of the new start-up businesses in operation today. The types of home businesses are as varied as people's talents and interests.

New technology has opened the door for Internet home business projects that were once impossible to operate in a home environment. Doing business online gives you the flexibility of being able to work from anywhere there's an Internet connection and at any time of the day or night.

Working for yourself out of your home allows for more flexibility for living, and some individuals, especially those with small children at home, find it easier to balance the demands of work and family. Many people enjoy the zero commute, decreased childcare costs, tax deductions, and not having to dress up for work every morning.

Be aware, however, that there are some downsides to working at home, such as staying focused, the tendency to overwork, and isolation from friends and family. Many people choose to remain at their current job until they build up their home business to the point where it can be operated on a full-time basis. If you do not consider yourself to be an organized, self-motivated, or disciplined individual, or you need the daily interaction of people, then working from home is not going to be the business for you. Carefully research and weigh the costs and benefits of owning your own business before you start. Although you will eliminate reporting to a boss, administrative red tape, and the other negatives of working for an employer, working for yourself will also eliminate receiving a guaranteed paycheck or any of the employer-sponsored benefits of paid vacation days, sick time, health and liability insurance, and a retirement plan.

However, if you have an entrepreneurial spirit and are brave enough to consider giving up your day job to start a new career or new business, go ahead and begin planning your business venture. Solicit plenty of professional advice before you quit your job or invest your life savings to ensure that your business will be a success. There are many sources of expertise and books written on the subject of starting your own business, from creating a business plan and securing financing to managing daily operations. These sources can be purchased from a bookstore, are available free of charge from your local library, or can be found online from such organizations as the Small Business Administration at www.sba.gov/smallbusinesssplanner/index. html. Many colleges and universities sponsor small business development centers that provide free business plan and funding advice to anyone interested in starting a small business.

If you are considering buying an established business and hiring employees, you will need to consider ways to raise or borrow sufficient start-up capital to pay the bills while you're waiting for that first paycheck to come in. Other considerations are obtaining the proper licenses and permits, furnishing your business with the necessary equipment to run your operation, marketing your products, paying taxes, hiring employees, purchasing insurance, handling legal concerns, and protecting your ideas or new inventions. However, if you have a good idea, carefully plan out each contingency of your business, and have the necessary perseverance and business savvy, you can be successful!

JOB SATISFACTION

To make a good decision about your future, it is important to recognize what it is that makes work satisfying to *you*. Job satisfaction is a highly personalized issue; what makes one job exciting to one person may make it totally boring to another. What people value in work is unique; some people value achievement, status, power, or recognition, whereas others value more social rewards like the relationships they form at work or whether their work is meaningful or important. Each of us needs to come up with our own definition of what makes a job satisfying. What factors are important to you? What motivates, inspires, or causes you to feel achievement, joy, or interest? For some people, work is not nearly as important as their home life, their children, family relationships, or their hobbies, music, art, or other part-time pursuits. Although their job may be enjoyable, it is not the center of their life but simply a way to pay the bills and allow them to pursue more important matters that exist outside of work. To others, work *is* their hobby or passion and occupies a central role in their life.

In the 1950s and 1960s, the psychologist Frederick Herzberg started looking at the issue of what people wanted from their jobs. He found that the factors that people attributed to satisfaction (achievement, recognition, the work itself, responsibility, advancement, growth) were different than what they attributed to dissatisfaction (company policies, supervision, relationship with supervisor and peers, work conditions, salary, status, security).[1] In other words, our reasons for *liking* our jobs have more to do with factors intrinsic to the work itself, and our reasons for *not liking* our jobs are usually related to the work environment.

A recent survey by *Salary.com* revealed that compensation was the most important factor when choosing to leave a job but was less of a factor for staying in a job. When broken down by gender, attractive compensation was the top reason for staying in a job for men, whereas women focused more on working relationships and desirable working hours.[2]

The following is a list of common work values that contribute to job satisfaction. Place a check mark next to the values that are most important to your job satisfaction and then rank them in order of importance.

___Job level	___Tenure in the organization
___Pay	___Promotion
___Security	___Fringe benefits
___Demographics	___Interpersonal relationships
___Supervision	___Relationship with supervisor/boss
___Coworkers	___The work itself
___Creativity	___Allowing you to do what you do best
___Complexity	___Interesting work
___Power	___Autonomy or independence
___Amount of travel	___Number of meetings
___Perceived status	___Importance or value of work
___Professionalism	___Variety
___Level of activity	___Level of challenge
___Gratifying work	___Working in teams
___Accomplishment	___Work schedule
___The organization	___Type or size of office
___Customer contact	___Availability of overtime

Order of Importance:

1. _____

2. _____

3. _____

4. _____

5. _____

If you are currently employed and are not satisfied with your work life, try to identify the source(s) of dissatisfaction. Make a list of the positive and negative aspects of your current job:

Current Position
Positives   Negatives

_____   _____
_____   _____
_____   _____
_____   _____

Now describe your ideal (or future) job using the following criteria:

1. Type of work (people, data, information, numbers, computers, tools, machines, animals, nature, plants)?

2. Type of employer (family owned, corporate, manufacturing, government, hospital, laboratory, more than 50 employees, less than 50 employees)?

3. Location (east coast, west coast, urban, rural, close to home, within 30 miles)?

4. Salary (hourly or annual amount, paid weekly, monthly, commission, bonuses)?

5. Benefits (health, dental, vision, retirement, car, mileage, company discount, other perks)?

6. Work schedule (day, night, part time, full time, flexible hours)?

7. Level of autonomy (independent, semi-independent, professional, management, staff, clerical, under someone's direct supervision)?

8. Physical work environment (office, classroom, hospital, laboratory, clinic, manufacturing plant, body shop, indoors, outdoors, travel to multiple locations, home)?

9. Amount of direct people contact (high customer or people contact, little customer or people interaction, customer contact by appointment only, interact only with coworkers)?

10. Workplace culture (relaxed or rigid, busy or slow, professional or informal, creative or structured, fun or serious, team-centered or autonomous, dress code, age/gender/personality of coworkers, culturally diverse)?

Compare the positive aspects of your current job with your ideal job. What do the results tell you about yourself and your work values? Uncovering the reasons behind job dissatisfaction can provide clues of where to proceed next in your life. For example, being stressed may indicate the need to cut back your hours or to find an occupation that is less stressful. Boredom, on the other hand, may indicate the need to find a job with more challenge or activity. I know a former controller of a large financial firm who became tired of the "rat race" and decided to indulge her love of music and technical ability by becoming a certified piano tuner. She is now not only much happier, but after simplifying her lifestyle, finds that her current income is more than adequate to meet her needs.

SOME FINAL CONSIDERATIONS

Despite the inherent anxiety involved in job change or making the decision to go back to school full time, most people find career and job change refreshing. Sure, you will probably miss some aspects of your old job and the companionship of your colleagues, but you can always continue those relationships beyond the work setting. Most people look forward to the prospect of facing new challenges and using a new set of skills in a different environment. They also enjoy the opportunity to be valued as a contributor in their new role rather than being taken for granted. When you feel better about your employment situation, everyone around you will benefit.

Although the future is an unknown quantity, you do know how you feel about your present situation. Do nothing and you will continue in that situation. Make a change, and at least you have the chance for creating a better and brighter future. Whatever your decision, make the decision that's right for you.

Chapter 7

Overcome Obstacles

What is the difference between a stumbling block and a stepping stone?
The way you approach it.

Maya Sullivan

Making a lifestyle change can be a frightening and difficult thing for many people. But the reality is that if we don't change, we will never move beyond our present situation. Many people are able to improve their jobs, their social life, and reach their goals. What makes the difference for those people is that they are able to move beyond their barriers. Barriers are obstacles that are perceived to be so real and impenetrable that they prevent people from taking some kind of action even though their logic may dictate otherwise. People who are able to work past their barriers are able to problem solve alternatives and solutions and move past those barriers.

We now live in a world where recareering and reeducating is an acceptable and even expected part of our adult career lives. We are all living longer and therefore working longer. Given the fact that most of us will live well into our eighties, the prospect of starting a new job or a new career at thirty or forty is now a very realistic scenario.

The time is going to go by anyway, whether you use that time going to school or continuing to work in your same old job. The question to ask yourself is—what do I want to *do* with that time?

The difficulty for most adults is that they have bills, house payments, children, spouses, and even elderly parents to care for and support. They have the added complication of life's expectations and responsibilities. Despite our adult responsibilities, I believe that doing work you enjoy for the remaining working years of your life, even if it means going back to school to do so, is a better alternative to staying in a low-paying or unhappy employment situation.

By now, most of you are probably saying to yourselves, "But I can't go back to school now, or leave my job because____" (you fill in the blank). But before you totally discard the idea of getting a new job or going back to school at your age because of your bills, where you live, and so on and so forth, let's take a few moments to examine some of the common "yes, buts" that prevent people from improving their lives and see whether we can't find some workable alternatives.

ALTERNATIVES TO COMMON "YES, BUTS ... "

■ "I can't afford to go back to school"

This is a very realistic concern for everyone. But have you applied for financial aid? Can you work and go to school part time, on weekends, or earn your degree through distance learning? There are many state and federal programs that offer monetary support (as well as academic support services) for individuals who fall into certain categories (e.g., single parents, displaced homemakers, people entering fields that are nontraditional to their gender). Investigate these possible funding sources by visiting your local One-Stop Career Center, assistance agency, or your local college or university's financial aid office. If you have been recently laid off, do you qualify for any retraining funding, such as the Trade Readjustment Act? Are there any special grants, loans, or scholarships available that you might qualify for?

■ "School takes too long"

The time is going to go by anyway, whether or not you go back to school.[1] Try to think of school as an investment in your, or your children's, future. Consider weekend programs, accelerated courses, fast track programs, credit for life experience, taking CLEP examinations in lieu of courses, or online degrees. Make an appointment with your local college or university's admissions office for more information about these educational options.

■ "I'll never be able to make it in college because I didn't get good grades in high school"

Look at the reason(s) *why* you didn't get good grades in high school. Was it because of lack of studying? Were your interests elsewhere? Chances are those reasons or circumstances no longer exist. The good news is that college is a chance for a fresh start. Many students who didn't do very well in high school end up excelling in college because they're more motivated, more mature, and more serious about their future.

■ "I'm too old to go back to school"

Colleges and universities have no age limit. In fact, many offer free classes or reduced tuition for individuals over sixty-two. Today, there are so many adult students attending school that they are no longer being called "nontraditional." Students over the age of twenty-five currently make up 39% of postsecondary students at colleges and universities,[2] and 46% of students at community colleges are at least twenty-five years old.[3] The National Center for Education Statistics projects that from 2005 to 2016 the number of students twenty-five and over will increase by 21%.[4] The chances are very good that about half your class will be made up of students as old, or older, than you.

■ "I don't know what I want to do"

In my experience, most people know (if they really look deep inside themselves) what they like and what they don't like. Some people have never had the opportunity to discover who they are or what they are good at because their career path was "chosen" for them at an early age, or they went right into marriage or a job without exploring any other options. Everyone goes through this self-discovery process at some point in their lives. A good career counselor can help you sort things out and identify career options. Even if you decide to begin school without having a clear picture of your career goals, you will still have time to change your major or adjust your plans.

■ "The program I want is only offered during the day"

Some programs, especially those with competitive entrance requirements (translated to mean these majors are in high demand), may only be offered during the traditional school day. You have no control over this. First of all, investigate whether there is another college or university within commuting distance that offers that program. Is it possible to earn a degree in that field via distance education? If not, what about the possibility of going to school during the day and working at night or on the weekends? Can you apply for enough financial aid to allow you to go to school full time? Are there any other funding options like scholarships, personal loans, or help from relatives? If you have to quit your job or work part time while going to school to make this work, remember that the financial sacrifice will only be for a short period of time. Think about how better off you will be in the long run.

■ "I'd like to go to school, but I have to work full time to keep my benefits"

This is a tough situation, especially if you are single and are the sole source of medical insurance. Is it possible to take classes at night, on the weekends, or by distance education? Would your employer allow you any flexibility to attend a class during the day? Could you find another job that would allow more flexible hours or allow you to work a second or third shift and take classes later in the morning or during the afternoon? This would need to be investigated thoroughly beforehand, of course. Many colleges offer a basic health insurance plan to students at a reduced rate. The risk may be worth it in the end, especially if you are able to get a job whose salary and benefit package is considerably better than what you have now.

■ "You have to get a bachelor's degree to earn a good living"

Although a four-year education is never wasted, there are many good paying occupations that do not require a four-year degree, such as health care and the skilled technology fields. Keep in mind that only about 20% of all openings require a bachelor's degree or more.[5] Securing a well-paying job in your chosen occupation depends on many factors, some of which you have no direct control over like the economy, the demand in the labor market, and advancements in technology. In today's world, there are no guarantees, but you can greatly increase your chances of employment through education and experience.

■ "What if I can't find a job when I graduate?"

In today's economy, there is no guarantee that *anyone* will get a job, but there are ways to dramatically increase your employability. The best way to prepare yourself for the future marketplace is to carefully research the employment forecasts of the career you are considering going back to school for. Discuss the employment or "placement" potential with the career services department at the college where you intend to enroll or look up the projected employment statistics reported by the U.S. Bureau of Labor Statistics. Again, how tolerable is doing nothing and staying at your present job?

■ "I don't have time to look for a new job (or finish my degree)"

Finding time, like everything else, is a matter of priority. Is there anything you can cut back on at this point in your life to free up even one extra hour a day to search for a job? Or take a class one night a week? Will your obligations or constraints on your time decrease in the future when your children start school, or you are finished teaching that class, or your husband or wife gets a job on first shift? If you are simply unable to find the time at this point in your life, is it possible to begin making plans to finish your degree or look for a new job in the future? When *will* getting a better job or earning your degree be a priority?

■ "I'm too old to get a job in ... "

That may have been true in our parents' world of work but not in today's job market. Labor shortages and the improved health of older Americans have made those old rules obsolete in many occupations today. Consider that the average lifespan in the U.S. has increased by thirty years since 1900. The average baby boomer, and there will be 6,000 people turning sixty each day in America, will live to their mid-eighties.[6] Today's sixty-year-old worker is just as vibrant and mentally sharp as their younger counterparts. The trick is to emphasize that you're physically and mentally able to work and have kept up with the latest technology (like computers).

Industries that are more "elder friendly" include retail, education, and health care. Shortages of workers in health care have caused employers to turn a blind eye to age and gender. In fact, I know of several individuals in their mid-fifties who recently graduated with degrees in nursing and were hired *before* they graduated. Some companies like CVS, which has pharmacies located all over the U.S., are offering "snowbird" programs to their employees who wish to spend the winter months in a warmer climate.

■ "You can only get a job by knowing someone"

Although unfortunately this still is true in many parts of the country, it isn't necessarily true everywhere. There are not enough politically connected individuals to fill all of the job openings. The fact is that most jobs are filled with people who are qualified and have the required skills. Granted, they may have used networking to their advantage to hear about an opening, or they may have brought their credentials to someone's attention before the job was advertised. Not all jobs are advertised in the newspaper, some are advertised by word of mouth referrals, so it pays to spread the word that you're looking and to keep on applying.

■ "I'll never be able to find another job in my field"

Are you absolutely sure, beyond the shadow of a doubt, that you will "never" find another job like the one you have? What would your life be like if this wasn't true? There are lots of jobs out there, and new ones are posted every day. If you have tried looking for another position, did you give yourself enough time to search for openings? Sometimes it takes several months to find a comparable position depending on the industry and the local labor market. As long as you are still employed, you have nothing to lose by continuing to look.

■ "That job is too far away, or doesn't pay enough, or is temporary, or . . . "

If you have the resources to wait for a job to come along that is better than one that is currently available, then by all means do so. But if your unemployment benefits have run out, and the prospects for finding another job are not very promising, then don't be so quick to rule out any job prospect. It's still a job, and some income is better than no income. Although this position may not be the one you want, it will allow you to pay a few bills, build up your skill set, and it may even provide you with a good reference while you continue to look for something better. If you are unable to find a full-time position, always consider taking part-time or temporary positions because these often have a very good chance of evolving into full-time permanent positions.

■ "There isn't anything I want to do (I don't like anything)"

Everyone likes to do something. Unless you truly do not want to work, you just haven't found the right job yet. Begin by taking an interest inventory to help you identify your interests, strengths, values, and personality type. If you "hate everything," you could be too burned out, disillusioned, tired, or angry to be able to see beyond your present situation. If you're not able to identify anything you *do* like, make a list of what you *don't* like and start with what's left. Then work with a career counselor, academic advisor, personal counselor, or some other professional to help you come up with a way to improve your life.

■ "I can't stand my current job, but I don't want to go back to school any longer than I have to, and I want to make the same salary I'm making now"

If you still enjoy your current job or profession, consider the possibility that you are in the right job but with the wrong employer. If that is the case, then your next course of action is to polish up your resume and canvass the job market for possible new employers. If you wish to enter a new field or type of work, consider any related professions or occupations that do not require any additional training but would benefit from your years of work experience (e.g., sales, customer service, some types of entry-level management, and entrepreneurship).

If you have some idea of the career you would like to pursue but are concerned about the length of schooling or your finances, consider the funding sources and accelerated programs discussed above. If you are unclear about which career to go into but are simply feeling an overwhelming desire to leave the job you're in, then taking some time to work on career planning and decision-making may be the best course of action.

If none of the above options are acceptable, you may want to talk with an employment recruiter, human resources professional, career counselor, or career coach to gain a broader perspective of what today's jobs require and what employers are looking for when filling these positions. If you find yourself left with little or no options, ask yourself if any of your constraints can be lifted, manipulated, or flexed in any way. You may need to brainstorm possibilities with your spouse, family members, or friends. Realize that with any decision there are no perfect solutions and there are upsides and downsides to every option, choice, and decision. What are you willing to do today to create the type of life you want tomorrow?

BELIEFS AND EXPECTATIONS

We are confronted with challenges and opportunities every day. Our ability to cope with challenging or threatening situations has a great deal to do with whether or not we believe we can create a successful outcome. Our *self-efficacy*, or how well we believe we can do something, has a great influence on our career development as well. Whether we reach our career goals can be helped or hindered by the self-efficacy beliefs that we hold. If we don't believe that we will be able to successfully reach our career goal, we will not be as motivated to try to achieve it.

Another factor that influences what we do is the beliefs we have about *why* things happen in the world. Each day, we are faced with decisions, tasks, and situations. Some of our efforts succeed, whereas others do not. What we attribute as the cause for our successes or failure is called *attribution theory*.[7] For example, we may feel that our situation in life is the result of internal factors, such as our natural abilities, intelligence, or hard work, or the result of outside factors such as sheer luck, fate, or world events.

If we believe our successes are the result of something that we can control, like our hard work, then we will be more motivated to try to solve our problems because we believe we can achieve them with a little effort and perseverance. Likewise, we may believe our failures are the result of our lack of ability. If we believe there is nothing we can do to improve our abilities, then we will take a very passive approach to what happens to us instead of trying to find a way to succeed: we believe it's "beyond our control."

Bernard Weiner determined that people tend to interpret the cause of an event as either (1) internal or external to our control (2) changeable or not over time; or (3) changeable or not by means of our own efforts.[8]

The attributions we make regarding why things happen and whether we have any control over what happens directly influence our future motivations and performance. People with a more optimistic attribution style tend to take on and overcome difficult situations because they believe they can positively influence the outcome. In other words, challenges are not viewed as insurmountable barriers. If we apply this same logic to career development, the barriers that stand in the way of reaching or achieving our career goals can be viewed as permanent roadblocks or as challenges that can be successfully overcome, depending on our perspective.

What is standing in your way from creating the kind of life you want? What are your roadblocks, obstacles, or constraints? How are you viewing these challenges? Do you believe you can change or improve any aspect of your situation? Are your roadblocks permanent obstacles that can't be moved, or can you find another way to move beyond that roadblock to reach your career goals? Can you creatively come up with any ways to make your current job situation more tolerable? Can you squeeze in a couple of classes on the weekend, earn your degree via distance education, start a home business after work hours, study in the afternoon while your kids are taking a nap, shift your work schedule around so you can attend class, or borrow some money from an uncle to pay for school to move closer to achieving your future desires, wishes, dreams, or goals?

Too many people feel stuck or trapped in a job they don't like, in a relationship that's not working, etc. Some take the necessary steps to overcome or change their situation, whereas others do not. Although there may be many reasons for why one person does something and another does not, fear is often the main reason that prevents people from creating the type of work life they would like. Fear of what the future will bring, fear of leaving the safety and comfort of a familiar situation (even if it is dull and boring), fear of stepping "outside of the box," fear of doing something on your own without the support or approval of your friends or family, fear of failing, fear of losing the time and money you invested, or even the fear of appearing foolish.

Once you identify or isolate the fears or concerns behind your particular "yes, buts," then you can begin to brainstorm alternatives. For some people, it is helpful to write down their fears, objections, concerns, and self-doubts on a piece of paper or even say them out loud to a trusted friend. Many fears lose their power when they're out in the open.

When I worked in the admissions office for a small campus, I would occasionally attend college fairs and other recruiting events. During these events, I'd talk to admissions recruiters from other competing colleges and universities. One time, an admissions representative from a local college came over and told me he always wanted to go into surveying (one of the degrees my institution offered). Over the course of several years, I saw this individual at different college fairs and he would repeat the same story. Then one day he got his finances in order, quit his job, and went back to school for his bachelor's degree. Today, he has a successful (and lucrative) job with a large surveying firm and says it was the best decision he ever made. Sure, juggling school, family, and financial responsibilities wasn't always fun, but in his case, the end result was worth the temporary hardship.

No one is advocating that you suddenly quit your job and give up everything you own to pursue your passion without any thought to the consequences. But with some creativity and careful planning, I'll bet you will be able to discover a workable alternative to allow you to pursue your goals. See if you can find a way to reach beyond your "yes, buts."

Chapter 8

Plan Your Career Strategically

If you really want to do something, you will find a way; if you don't, you'll find an excuse.

Unknown

Now that you have identified your priorities, explored your options, and overcome your "yes, buts," it's time to choose a direction and develop a plan of action.

In previous chapters, you identified your interests, strengths, skills, values, and any skills that need to be upgraded. Now, let's take a look at the big picture. Spend some time thinking about what you want to accomplish in your life. What things are important to you? Owning a large home? Having a lot of money? Close family relationships? Becoming an expert in your profession? Retiring early? Think about where you want to be ten, fifteen, or twenty years from now. Finally, what is your personal definition of success, and how will you know when you have reached it?

Many people just float through life without any definite plan. They drift from one job or one relationship to another or base their decisions on what others think they should do instead of on what they want to do. This chapter asks you to be in charge of your future by making decisions, setting goals, and developing a plan of action to reach those goals.

Begin by asking yourself what it is that makes you happy. What would your life have to be like to make you feel satisfied and full? What is important to you? What do you want to accomplish before you die? What is on your "Bucket List"? These are thought-provoking questions that shouldn't be answered casually. They require time and reflection. Keep in mind that values, aspirations, and life goals may change over time. What was important to you in your twenties may not be as important to you today. Life's situations, good and bad, have a way of shaping our priorities and providing us with a broader perspective on life.

Some people are so worried about making the wrong choice that they make no choice at all. Because there is no crystal ball to predict how our lives will turn out, the only thing we can do is make the best decision we can with the information we have at the time and try to prepare for any contingencies as best as we can. "Taking a chance" will be far less risky if you have a good plan in place to begin with. Making a decision doesn't mean you can't change your mind sometime down the road. A part of good strategic planning is to periodically reassess your situation to make sure the direction you have chosen is still the one in which you want to continue. And always remain open to new opportunities and situations.

Successful people do not spend their time fighting change. Instead, they embrace change and try to use it to their advantage. If preparations are made in advance, then when something does change you will be that much closer to finding another job because you will already have the proper networks in place to adapt to the change. In other words, you will be better equipped to move forward no matter what situation arises. Being caught unaware usually happens when a person did not even consider the possibility that something may change in the future. That's why many individuals who are laid off from their jobs are totally unprepared for the event and unprepared for what to do next.

Strategic Career Planning

Strategic planning has been used in the business world for some time. In business, all decisions and actions are based on reaching specific goals designed to accomplish the company's over-arching mission. Strategic plans begin with a focus on the organization's mission (its vision and/or values), goals to work toward the mission, strategies to achieve the goals, and a detailed plan of action with time limits to determine who will do what and by when.

A strategic plan should not be confused with a business plan. Business plans are much more detailed and focus on the first five years of a business's operation. Strategic plans, in contrast, are oriented toward the future growth and development of a company and are usually written with three- to five-year timelines, dictating a company's direction and action five to ten years in the future.

Traditionally, the strategic planning process begins by identifying strengths and weaknesses. Because you have already begun this process in the preceding chapters, you are now ready to move to the personal mission statement step of the strategic planning process. Once you have selected your career goal, even if in broad terms, the direction, method, and means of accomplishing your goal will begin to fall into place. You will then be able to identify what skills, training, education, job experience, and accomplishments you will need to acquire to practice in your profession or successfully market yourself to a company or organization. As we apply the concepts of business planning to career planning, your mission statement is your future career or professional goals. The steps that you take to find a new job, or go back to school to earn your degree, will be written in as the short- and long-term goals and objectives (complete with timelines and end dates), which are thoughtfully and strategically designed to enable you to fulfill your personal mission statement.

There are four basic steps involved in creating a strategic career plan. Each step will be discussed in more detail throughout this chapter.

I. Write a mission statement (career goal)

II. Develop goals and objectives (action plan)

III. Implement the plan (put your plan into action)

IV. Periodically review and revise your plan (review your progress and make any changes to your plan as needed)

I. WRITE A PERSONAL MISSION STATEMENT

Write a personal mission statement summarizing your long-term career goals. Your mission statement can be as long or as short as you like. Examples include, "Become a best-selling author of a children's book," "Complete my bachelor's degree in special education and secure a position in the community working with autistic children and their families," or "Work as an accountant with a large public accounting firm for five to ten years before opening a private practice as a certified public accountant in downtown Chicago." Sometimes it helps to develop a mental picture or image of yourself and your career over the next few years. Then describe that picture in detail on a sheet of paper or computer screen.

This step assumes that you have already completed the self-assessment and career decision-making steps in Chapter 5 and have chosen a desired course of action. If you are still unsure of your career goal, review Chapter 5 or make an appointment with a career counselor to take an interest inventory and develop a career plan.

II. DEVELOP GOALS AND OBJECTIVES

Outline the steps you will need to complete to reach your goal—including a timeline or completion dates.

Research

What information do you need to better understand your career options or how to prepare for your career goal? Make a checklist of the kinds of information you need and check each item off when you find it.

Gather the information you collected from your self-assessment in Chapter 5 and the work skills and values assessments you completed in Chapter 4. Then, see how closely they match your new career or work goal. If you are not as familiar with a particular career as you need to be, do some more research and then compare your results.

In terms of your skills and experience, how do your current skills compare with what is required for your future career? How will you obtain those qualifications? If you plan to go back to school to obtain those skills, or change your career, what degree or credentials are needed to practice in your career of choice? Research your chosen career field and identify the specific educational requirements and credentials required and the educational options available to help you obtain those credentials.

How to research schools

When developing an educational plan to go back to school, here are some of the things to consider:

- Type of school. Is it a community college, university, two-year or four-year school, local or out of state, public or private?
- Size. Consider the physical size as well as the number of students and faculty.
- Student composition. Is the school predominately male, female, or co-ed? What are the number of adult students and the percentage of full-time, part-time, day, or evening students? What is the diversity of the student population?
- Geographic location. Is the college in a rural or urban setting, within traveling distance or on a bus route?

- Availability of your major. Does the school offer your major? Are minors available? Does the school award certificates, associate or baccalaureate degrees? Does it offer graduate courses? What is the educational reputation of your intended degree among employers?

- Course offerings. Are courses offered primarily during the day in traditional lecture format or are they also offered at night, on Saturdays, on the weekends, at different locations, or online?

- Childcare. Are there any childcare facilities on or off campus?

- Student support services. Does the college offer tutoring, academic counseling, computer labs, a library, a cafeteria, and student organizations at convenient hours?

- Cost. What is the cost of tuition, books, and fees? Does the college offer a payment plan? Can you use a credit card? What is the cost of any additional student, lab, or activity fees or course supplies?

- Financial aid. What is the possibility of obtaining financial aid, work study, scholarships, on-campus employment, or other sources of financial help?

College tuition costs tend to increase each year, so plan for these accordingly in your budget. Make a list of possible colleges or universities that offer the major you have chosen. Then, gather as much information as possible about each college by viewing its website or visiting it in person. A list of educational web resources is located in Appendix B.

To make good long-term planning decisions about your career, you need to know what the employment outlook is going to be for the career you are considering. Research the companies and employers who hire employees in your intended career field and where they are located. Look up the labor market forecast for your particular career. Investigate the average starting salary in your geographic area and how many openings are available each year.

If you intend to reenter the job market or change jobs, research the employers hiring in your particular area and the starting and average salaries for your field. Will you be earning more or less in your new career? What is your potential for advancement or promotions? If you are considering relocating, factor in any cost-of-living differences. Living expenses such as housing or renting costs, property taxes, food, fuel, and utilities vary greatly from state to state and across the country. Moving from a small rural town to a metropolitan city may negate any increase in salary you may receive after you add everything up. A list of salary and cost-of-living web resources is listed in Appendix B.

How to research companies and employers

When researching a company or employer consider the following:

- History of the company
- Product lines
- Customers
- Organizational structure
- Location of corporate headquarters
- Size of the company
- Number of employees
- Holdings and annual sales growth for past five years
- Reputation or standing in the industry
- Potential for growth

There are many places to find information about prospective employers and companies. One reliable source is Hoover's Online at www.hooversonline. com. Hoover's is a widely respected service that provides detailed information on over 50,000 public and private companies. Dunn & Bradstreet, www.dnb. com, is another excellent resource that provides information on public and private companies by size, location, and industry.

It is generally easier to find information about publicly owned companies than privately owned ones. To find out whether a company is a subsidiary of a larger parent organization, is privately owned, or is foreign owned, look at the *Directory of Corporation Affiliations* by National Register Publishing. Other good sources of information are *America's Corporate Families* by Dun & Bradstreet, *Standard and Poor's Register of Corporations, Directors, and Executives, Volume 3*, and *Who Owns Whom: North American Edition* by Dun & Bradstreet. To find information about small, local, or regional companies, check to see whether the company has a website or inquire about the company at your local chamber of commerce.

Develop Goals and Objectives

Goals are useful tools to help you succeed. Goals do not have to be elaborate, but they do need to be oriented toward the future and preferably something that you can realistically obtain, such as saving up for a new boat or learning how to play golf. An unrealistic goal might be winning the lottery or learning to play golf as well as Tiger Woods. Once a goal is selected, then a course of action is laid down to achieve that goal.

Goal setting can be helpful if you are not used to operating in this manner or have trouble staying motivated. Setting short-term goals can also help you organize your present situation. People who are successful on weight loss programs arm themselves with some type of structured program, set reasonable weight loss goals over a period of time, or make a pact with a partner to help them achieve their weight loss. Having a goal doesn't mean you have to be a slave to it either. These are your goals and are subject to change as the situation dictates.

Goals are usually broken down into short-term and long-term goals. Objectives are the steps along the way to reach each short-term and long-term goal. Short-term goals focus on the present to the next few weeks or years. They should be concrete, specific, measurable, and something that you can realistically accomplish in the near future. Examples of short-term goals include going to school or finding a job (including the tasks of drafting a resume, cover letter, and references, identifying employers, applying, interviewing, and accepting a first job). Your objectives to reach those goals may include applying to college, taking classes, writing a resume, and participating in an internship in the summer. Other short-term goals may include working for three to five years, building experience or skills, developing a particular area of expertise, seeking a promotion, continuing your education, making contacts in the professional community, or seeking out and applying for other positions until you reach your career destination.

Long-term goals are more general and usually span a period of five or more years. Long-term goals are focused on the future. An example of a long-term goal may be to own your own business, whereas a short-term goal is to work at your current job until you can save enough money to buy that store or office space. Another long-term goal may be to get a job teaching science at the local high school, whereas a short-term goal would be to go back to school to earn your teaching degree in biology, do your student teaching at your local high school, pass your state certification examination, and apply for a job in the science department.

Create a budget

Whether you decide to go back to school or search for a new job, it's a good idea to factor in your expenses. If you are going back to school, include travel costs to and from school, tuition, fees, books, food, and daily living expenses. Do you need to purchase a computer or are computers available on campus in a computer lab? Is the library open extended hours or only during the day? Do you have Internet access from home to access your registration information or the library's databases? If you are going to take any online classes, do you need a high-speed Internet connection?

Create a budget to prepare for job hunting expenses. Include the costs of a new interviewing wardrobe, a new hairstyle, postage, fax transmissions, or long-distance phone calls when applying for positions. Don't forget mileage, taxi fare, or airfare to and from interviews. Don't assume that the company you are interviewing with will reimburse you for travel expenses. Even if they will cover your costs, you may need to have money up front to book a hotel or airline flight while you wait to be reimbursed. If you are interviewing out of state, factor in mileage, the cost of a rental car or airfare, and hotel accommodations. Generally, any meals during the interview period will be covered but don't forget about meals before and after the interview.

If you plan to relocate, calculate the cost of household moving expenses, fees involved in buying and selling your home, and fees for shipping household goods. Also, include the cost of a hotel while you are looking for a house or apartment. Some of these moving expenses may be tax deductible.

III. IMPLEMENT YOUR PLAN

Now put your plan into action. The following are three examples of career, educational, and employment plans for people in different stages of their careers.

Example 1

Career Goal: *Become a pediatric nurse in the new pediatric wing of the hospital in my hometown.*

Interests: *Working with children, computer programming, enjoy science and anatomy.*

Skills: *Compassionate, people oriented, organized, computer literate.*

Skills or Credentials Needed: *Registered nursing degree, state license.*

Educational Plan:

1. **School:** *Enroll in local community college thirty miles away this fall semester.*
2. **Degree:** *Earn my associate's degree in nursing within three years.* (Include an outline of courses for each semester.)
3. **Finance Plan A:** *Apply for and obtain scholarships from local hospital to finance tuition and books.*
4. **Finance Plan B:** *Apply for financial aid and work on weekends.*

Employment Strategy:

1. *Take as many pediatric-related courses and obtain as many clinical experiences as possible.*
2. *Volunteer in local hospital over Christmas holiday and during spring break.*
3. *Create a resume, cover letter, and list of references.*
4. *Attend the college career fair to apply for a position.*

Example 2

Career Goal: *Establish a landscaping business specializing in water garden design.*

Action Steps:

1. *Continue working for five more years as a groundskeeper at the park.*
2. *Take one water garden specialty course at night each semester until complete certification in two years.*
3. *Develop side business of creating water garden landscaping for clients during evenings and on weekends.*
4. *Meet with small business development center to develop a business plan.*
5. *Meet with the bank to secure loan for start-up costs of establishing business.*
6. *When referrals reach two to three clients per month, retire from daytime position at the park and open full-time water garden business.*

Example 3

Long-Term Goal: *Senior graphic designer at a progressive advertising company with a salary of $80,000 per year and full medical, dental, and life insurance.*

Short-Term Goal: *Secure a job as an entry-level junior graphic designer to gain industry experience.*

Action Steps to Achieve Short-Term Goal:

1. *Create resume, cover letter, and list of references highlighting my career change.*
2. *Create a portfolio of twenty pieces of my best work to show an employer during the interview.*
3. *Apply for all job openings by using newspaper sources, word-of-mouth referrals, and online employment search engines.*

4. *Contact possible employers and inquire about possible openings.*

5. *Practice answering interview questions with a friend.*

6. *Buy new interviewing attire and create portfolio.*

Action Steps to Achieve Long-Term Goal:

1. *Work three to five years as a junior graphic designer to hone skills and learn everything I can about the graphic design field.*

2. *Search for a job at an advertising agency or take advanced graphic design/art or computer programming courses at night.*

3. *Find a mentor in my field or join a local graphic design professional organization to gain networking contacts.*

Sometimes you have to be very creative in brainstorming possibilities. Every situation has several possible options even though you may not like all of the options. Each of us make choices and compromises every day, from what clothes to wear in the morning to the type of dressing to put on our salad at dinner. Some choices and compromises are just more difficult to make than others. Ultimately, it comes down to the issue of deciding which inconveniences you are willing to live with in the short-term to benefit later on. Gather all of the facts to make the best possible decision. Consult with professional staff at colleges or universities because they may be able to suggest some solutions you may not have thought of. Continue to work toward your goal. Find something you can do today, tomorrow, next week, or next year.

Pretend for the moment that you've always wanted to be a medical illustrator. Assume that you have some moderate art ability and some familiarity of anatomy and physiology from your science courses in college. Since that time, you have been working in retail, raising a family, and taking private art lessons one night a week. You draw in your spare time and sometimes enter art fairs or contests. You wonder what's required to be an art illustrator. After doing some research, you find that some kind of formal art training plus knowledge of anatomy and physiology, some work experience, and a killer portfolio are needed to break into the profession. So you decide to go to school at night and pick up some basic anatomy and physiology classes. With the cooperation of your art instructor, you target your art lessons on human anatomy and work on extra assignments to build your skills. Then you apply for an internship or volunteer to work at a medical college preparing illustrated anatomic study guides for first-year medical students. Through your contacts at the college, you acquire a freelance job with a textbook publishing company to do the artwork for an upcoming anatomy book. Because you are unable to locate a full-time position, you also start giving art lessons at your local art studio, which you discover you love doing. Eventually, you land a teaching position in the art department at your local college. Meanwhile, your reputation begins to build and you start receiving offers to do a series of freelance jobs with a major medical publishing company. Eventually, you launch your own website and realize your dream.

I used to work with a woman who wanted to transition away from the personal counseling field into career counseling. She already held a master's degree in counseling (the minimum educational requirement for the position) and had previous counseling and academic advising experience from previous positions in the mental health and college settings. But she wasn't up to date in career counseling strategies and techniques. So she took as many individual and group career courses as were offered at a local college at night and over the summer, offered to see more students with career issues at her job just for the experience, and reviewed the latest career development literature to brush up on the latest theories, terminology, and techniques in the field. When a position in the career services department came along, she was able to successfully compete for that career counseling position because she could demonstrate her new skills and expertise in that area.

IV. PERIODICALLY REVIEW AND REVISE YOUR PLANS

Many action plans fail because there was no evaluative measure built into the action plan. In other words, there was no checkpoint from which to propel the plan from one step to the other and no way to determine whether, or when, a goal had been met. In business, if you do not reach your sales goal, the company loses money, which sets off a whole cascade of unfortunate consequences (like having to lay people off). Weight loss programs do not work simply by saying "I'm going to lose weight." Without specifying how much weight, like five pounds each month until I am twenty pounds lighter, all the good intentions in the world will end up just fading away over time.

Assigning dates to your action steps will force you to stay on track and will ultimately help you reach your goals. It will also help you measure your progress (or lack of progress). Periodically reassess your situation and revise your action steps as necessary. Whether you add or delete steps, change, revise, or rebalance your plan, monitor your progress and reward yourself for the steps you have accomplished.

Developing a Career Portfolio

Although a portfolio is often used as a job search tool, it can also be used as a career planning and educational tool. Many college programs require their students to create a portfolio during the course of their studies to help evaluate and document their progress. After graduation, a portfolio then serves as an invaluable tool to demonstrate education, skills, competencies, and experience to a prospective employee.

Here are a few basic suggestions to help you start thinking about how to put your portfolio together and how to use it. Gather together examples and documentation of your accomplishments and skills, assignments, internships, special training, workshops, volunteer work activities, committees served on, papers, classroom projects, and laboratory assignments completed, and other activities in your life. Also include any results of career or educational planning such as results of interest inventories, a career or goals statement, etc. Here are some possible items to include:

- Sample resume and cover letter
- Results of interest inventories
- Occupational or informational research
- Statement of career goals or educational plan
- Personal mission or philosophy statement
- Copies of academic transcripts
- Awards, honors, diplomas, degrees, certificates, and licenses
- Letters of reference or commendation from former teachers and employers
- Writing samples
- Internships, co-op experiences, study abroad or volunteer experiences (provide statements from supervisors)
- Laboratory reports, research projects, papers submitted for publication in professional journals
- Copies of research papers, lesson plans, computer programs, websites, class projects, proposals, or other innovative or outstanding classroom assignments
- Copies of any artistic or creative work like music compositions, photographs, digital recordings, recordings of dance, musical, or theatre productions
- Pictures of any large item you designed, created, or built such as sculptures, paintings, carpentry projects, buildings, water gardens, floral designs, clothing, fabrics, or architectural designs
- Sporting awards
- Documentation of leadership experience

- Agendas of meetings you conducted
- Flyers or other promotional materials you designed
- Positive evaluations received from teachers or clinic or internship supervisors
- Performance reviews or job evaluations, rating forms, work samples, records of promotions, employee awards or honors, written proposals, or strategic plans
- Evidence of membership or offices held in any professional or community organizations
- Grant proposals written or received
- Certificates of attendance at seminars, workshops, or conferences
- Evidence of talks, speeches, or presentations given at conferences or workshops
- Travel experiences, countries visited, artifacts gathered
- Anything that adds value to or is going to elicit additional conversation during the interview

These categories are a guide to get you started. Use some or all of the categories as appropriate. Feel free to create additional sections of your portfolio as you feel necessary. Your portfolio is a visual representation of who you are and what you can bring to a company or organization. Don't be afraid to highlight ALL aspects of your skills!

When you are in the workforce, continue to develop and build upon your portfolio as you progress in your career. Incorporate any work you've done that relates to what you have learned on the job. As you change positions throughout your career or as you apply for promotions, review your portfolio before each interview and add or delete items as appropriate to match the needs of the employer. A portfolio can be a real confidence booster as you review past accomplishments and achievements.

Chapter 9

Remember: It's Never Too Late to Go Back to School

Through learning we re-create ourselves. Through learning we become able to do something we were never able to do.

Peter Senge

THE VALUE OF EDUCATION

During the 1950s and 1960s, a high school diploma was enough to guarantee a good paying job. Manufacturing jobs were able to provide a middle-class lifestyle for many high school–educated workers. Although manufacturing employment peaked in 1979, it has declined ever since. Over the years, the declines in manufacturing employment have been offset by gains in service-providing industries.[1] This economic shift, coupled with rapid changes in technology and the advent of the Internet, required a more educated workforce to perform a majority of the jobs in the twenty-first century. Today, some type of college education is necessary to secure a job with family-sustaining wages.

Next to buying a home, a college degree is one of the largest investments you will make. Although going to college can be expensive, it is a worthwhile investment in your future. The long-term payoffs include more career options, better promotion opportunities, higher earnings, and lower unemployment. In today's challenging economic times, education may also be the only way to deal with labor market fluctuations.

According to data released by the U.S. Bureau of Labor Statistics, average earnings increase at every level of education. In 2005, people who finished high school earned almost $75 more each week as compared with those who dropped out. People who completed an associate degree earned more than $100 as compared with high school graduates.[2]

If you have no education beyond high school, you will need some kind of college degree or technical training to enter a new career field or to advance at your workplace. Supervisors considering candidates for promotion tend to look more favorably upon those who have a college degree than on those who do not have one.

Good-paying occupations that require an associate degree, apprenticeship, or a short-term training program are the skilled trades (plumbing, HVAC, electrical, automotive, truck driving, carpentry, diesel mechanics, police, executive and legal secretary, cosmetology, medical billing, and computer support technology).

Several of the allied health professions such as registered nursing, respiratory therapy, radiology, dental hygiene, paramedics, medical laboratory technology, and veterinary technology allow graduates to become registered or licensed professionals with a two-year degree and satisfactory completion of a certifying examination. However, if these individuals want to move into a management position, then they must have at least a bachelor's degree. If they want to teach at a college or university, then a master's degree is required in their respective discipline.

Many professional jobs (education, accounting, actuarial science, business logistics, meteorology, engineering, and communications) consider a bachelor's degree the entry-level minimum, whereas others require a master's, doctoral, or professional degree (nurse anesthetist, chiropractor, counselor, psychologist, college professor, veterinarian, pharmacist, and librarian).

There are a number of occupations that require at least a bachelor's degree and some related work experience but that do not require a specific major. These include account executive, college administrator, customer service representative, editorial assistant, FBI/CIA special agent, fund-raiser, insurance agent, legislative advocate, loan officer, management trainee, manufacturer's sales representative, marketing research staff, police officer, private investigator, public relations worker, publishing agent, educational sales consultant, retail store manager, sales representative, travel agent, underwriter, and writer.

In general, the more education you have, the easier it is to transition into a new career. However, there are exceptions. Each profession has its own particular professional standards and educational requirements, which are not necessarily consistent across occupations. For example, the starting salary for someone with an associate degree in nursing can be higher than the starting salary for someone with a bachelor's degree. But to teach nursing courses at a college or university, you must have at least a master's degree, and preferably a doctorate. Therefore, it is important to do your research and find out what the educational, certification, or licensure requirements are for the career or occupation you are interested in.

The current labor market demand is another important variable that will inflate or deflate the starting salary of a particular occupation. Nursing wasn't always the highly sought after, high-paying profession it is today. The severe nationwide shortage of nurses, plus a growing aging population, has created an unprecedented demand for nurses. In response, the health care industry has increased salaries, benefits, and sign-on bonuses in an attempt to attract and retain nursing professionals. Being aware of economic conditions and future career trends is important in determining the future labor market supply and demand for jobs in your particular geographic area.

If you always wanted to have a particular profession, but for whatever reason could not commit to the length of schooling involved, there are plenty of alternatives available that you may find just as satisfying. For example, I have worked with people who told me they always wanted to become a counselor but were unable or unwilling to go to school for the length of time required to earn a master's degree (the required degree in that profession). The next best option is to find a career with a shorter training period that will allow them to work with and help people. Many professional programs such as physical therapy, occupational therapy, medical technology, education, and nursing have two-year counterparts (aide positions). Once in the workforce, there is always the option of continuing your schooling to complete the professional degree.

I once worked with a young man who wanted to go into accounting. Although his ultimate goal was to become a CPA, he couldn't afford to go to school for four years because of family obligations. Because he really enjoyed his accounting classes, he decided to begin his career by completing a one-year accounting certificate. This gave him the minimal amount of training to land a job with an accounting firm during the upcoming tax season. When the tax season ended, the company kept him on and he continued to go to school during the evening to earn his associate degree in accounting technology. This young man was able to pursue the career he enjoyed, meet his family obligations, and still has the option of working toward his bachelor's degree and becoming a CPA if he chooses to in the future.

ISSUES FACING ADULT STUDENTS

Adult students are the fastest-growing educational demographic. According to the U.S. Department of Education, only 28% of all college students were twenty-five years of age or older in 1970. In 1998, that number had increased to 41%. Today, the average age of a student attending a community college is twenty-nine years.[3] Another interesting trend is that more women than men are enrolling in college, and that number continues to increase. According to the National Center for Education Statistics, women are projected to earn 58% of the bachelor's degrees and 61% of the master's degrees awarded in 2007 to 2008.[4] In addition, women are projected to earn more doctoral degrees and more first-professional degrees such as in law, dentistry, pharmacy, chiropractic therapy, and medicine.[5]

Students in their twenties, thirties, and forties have a different set of issues than traditional eighteen-year-olds. Both age groups worry about finding a major they enjoy, the length of time it will take to graduate, and whether they'll be able to support themselves after graduation. However, adult students have the additional complications of age, family, and financial responsibilities. They are concerned about making their mortgage payments on time, balancing family and school, raising their children, and a myriad of other responsibilities that most eighteen-year-olds have yet to experience. Some adult students went straight into the workforce after high school and are trying to make the adjustment back into academia. Others are single parents trying to juggle school and home in an attempt to make a better life for themselves and their children, and still other adult students are just taking a few classes here and there to better position themselves for promotions at work.

Students are as nervous about starting school at forty as they are at eighteen years old. I recently listened to an adult student describe how at fifty-two she was concerned about sitting in class with a bunch of teenagers. She had to learn to get down to their level, but once she did, she fit right in. During those first few weeks, she didn't know if she would be able to do college work, but her professors encouraged her because they saw her potential. She eventually graduated with her bachelor's degree and is beginning a master's program.

Adult students begin school with many doubts: Can I do this? Should I be doing this? Am I neglecting my family? How will I find the time to get everything done? Will my family understand? Will they support me? Am I smart enough to be successful in college? What will the other students in the class think of me? Will I fit in?

Balancing the demands of school, marriage, work, and family responsibilities is critical. Finding enough time to work, study, make the meals, pick up the kids from school activities, and spend quality time with them is critical in making going back to school work. Having a backup baby-sitting plan is critical in case the baby-sitter becomes ill or has to take a day off. Family members need to become comfortable with a new routine that may involve some temporary inconveniences such as having to prepare dinner because mom or dad has a late class, or finding a ride home after soccer practice because mom has to study for an exam, or learning to abide by a quiet time after dinner when everyone does their homework.

If you're a single parent attending school on a part-time or full-time basis, daycare is going to be a major issue. Some colleges offer tuition assistance for subsidized daycare, others have on-campus daycare centers, and some even provide on-campus housing for parents and their children. Check out these options at the college where you intend to apply. If the college you want to attend does not have a daycare center, and your income is limited, you may qualify for subsidized housing through your local county assistance office. Other options are to enroll your child in private daycare or find a relative or neighbor who is willing to watch your children.

Many adult students delayed attending college after high school because they made the decision to put their spouse through school or stayed home and raised their children. Now that their marital status has changed, or their children are in school or have graduated, it's their turn. If it has been several years since you attended school, the best advice for success is, *start slow*! Begin by enrolling in only one course, preferably something you enjoy. Once you get back into the rhythm of attending class and studying for exams, you can pick up the credit load.

At the community college where I work, we offer a grant-funded program for single parents returning to the workforce and another program for welfare recipients attending college. The majority of the participants are single women. These students come from very different backgrounds and circumstances. Some are divorced, some widowed, and others have recently earned their GED. Despite their differences, most of these women (and men) say the reason they chose to enroll in college is to be able to get a job that will allow them to create a better life for themselves and their children. Many of these women have said that their children are the reason they enrolled in school. These parents attend school during the day, work on weekends, manage a household, take care of their young children, and study at night after the children go to bed. Interestingly, several have said that since they've gone back to college, they've noticed that their children have been doing better in school. The children see mom doing her homework at night and have started to follow her example. What a wonderful legacy for the entire family!

PAYING FOR SCHOOL

Many companies now offer tuition reimbursement benefits for their employees. Some pay all tuition costs, others pay a percentage, and others pay a certain amount depending on the pay grade the employee earns. Check with the human resources department at your place of work to see what tuition reimbursement benefits your company offers.

If you have been laid off because your company closed or moved overseas, you may be eligible for Trade Act Assistance (TAA) benefits. TAA programs cover tuition and books as well as continue to provide unemployment benefits while you attend school (usually for a maximum of two years). This program is offered through your local unemployment office, now known as a One-Stop Career Center.

There are many sources of federal, state, and local financial assistance. Financial aid is available in three forms: grants and scholarships (which do not have to be repaid), loans (must be repaid), and work study (campus based employment). The majority of financial aid is funded by the federal government (examples are the Pell Grant and Stafford Loan Programs), whereas other sources of student aid are funded through your state or your local college or university.

Federal grants and loans are usually awarded to the most financially needy applicants, whereas scholarships are usually awarded to individuals who demonstrate academic achievement. Student loans are now available to anyone, regardless of income level, and repayment is usually spread out over a ten-year period of time. Money is awarded on an annual basis; half is disbursed in the fall semester, and the remaining half is disbursed in the spring semester. As a general rule of thumb, financial aid is not available for the summer. However, there are a few exceptions that can be explained by the financial aid staff at your local college or university.

The federal work-study program is a great option that often goes unused. Students are limited to working twenty hours per week but can choose what campus office or department they would like to work in. Some students work in the admissions office giving tours to prospective students, others work in the computer lab, or the athletic department or library. The best part about work-study programs is that you earn as you learn. This means you can earn as little or as much of the dollar amount you're awarded each semester, and when there is no work to do, you can spend the time studying.

College- and university-based scholarships are created by benefactors in memory of a loved one, for students in a particular major, or to help a specific population of students (e.g., inner-city youth who intend to pursue a major in health care). Each scholarship has its own set of requirements that must be met to become eligible and may range from several hundred dollars to several thousand. There is usually an application process involved. Because many scholarships remain unawarded each year, it is well worth your while to take the time to search through the scholarship listings and fill out the applications. Most colleges and universities have active alumni and foundation programs, so students should be able to find a scholarship that matches their particular personal and academic circumstances.

If you are a veteran or a dependant of a veteran, you may qualify for military aid. Contact your local veteran's office or your school's financial aid office. If you don't qualify for financial aid or you still need to borrow more than the federal student loan limits allow, there are always educational loans available from commercial lenders. These rates are usually one or two percentage points higher than on federal student loans but are a good alternative if you don't qualify for anything else.

In addition to financial aid, students and their families now have access to several federal tax benefits that help lower college expenses. Examples of these are tax credits such as the Hope Scholarship tax credit, special saving accounts, and certain allowable deductions for the interest paid on student loans or for tuition and fees.

Applying for financial aid can be confusing and time consuming. Luckily, most states allow students to apply for federal and state financial aid through one application that can be conveniently completed online. This application is called the *Free Application for Federal Student Aid* (FAFSA) and can be found at www.fafsa.ed.gov. The official FAFSA site is a government site not a .com site. If you use a .com site you will probably be asked to pay a fee to submit the FAFSA, so use the official government site to submit your application free of charge. Student Aid on the WEB at www.studentaid.ed.gov is another good source of information about financial aid. There are many good websites on the Internet that allow you to search for available scholarships and other sources of funding. All of this information is available to the public free of charge, if you know where to look for it. With that said, be very cautious about any scholarship search service that charges a fee for their services.

It is a good idea to have your income tax returns completed before you begin the FAFSA application process and pay close attention to deadlines. Money is generally distributed on a first-come, first-served basis, so applying early is very important to receive all of the money that you are eligible for. The federal government will base your aid eligibility on last year's tax records. If you plan to reduce your hours or stop working to attend school, or you are now unemployed, your income will be less than what you made last year. Bring this to the attention of the school's financial aid director. They are authorized to take special circumstances into account and, where appropriate, may be able to rebalance aid awards. If you need help filling out the application or have any questions about the application or awarding process, most colleges and universities offer plenty of assistance by providing information on their websites, offering financial aid workshops, or providing financial aid personnel to answer your questions. College staff will not fill out the application form for you, but they will explain the process and answer any questions you may have.

WHICH COLLEGE TO ATTEND

Depending on whether you decide to enroll in a public or private college, a four-year university, or a community college or technical school, all of them will require an admissions application. In general, four-year universities and colleges, whether private or public, have a large number of majors to choose from, whereas technical schools or community colleges will be more specialized in their offerings. Community colleges offer two-year associate degree programs that are career oriented in nature as well as general courses that will transfer to a four-year institution.

Accreditation is an important consideration. There are two basic types of educational accreditation: (1) institutional and (2) specialized or programmatic. Institutional accreditation applies to an entire institution, whereas specialized or programmatic accreditation applies to programs, departments, or schools that are part of an institution. Most two- and four-year private and public colleges and universities are accredited by one of the six regional accrediting associations that accredit colleges and universities in the U.S. (Middle States Association, New England Association, North Central Association, Northwest Association, Southern Association, and Western Association of Schools and Colleges). Many private two-year business or technical schools are accredited by the *Accrediting Council for Independent Colleges and Schools* or the *Accrediting Commission of Career Schools and Colleges of Technology*. Online or distance education programs are often accredited by the *Accrediting Council for Continuing Education and Training* or the *Distance Education and Training Council*.

Keep in mind that some colleges and universities will accept credits only from institutions with similar accrediting bodies. If you are planning to transfer courses from a technical or business school to a college or university, check with the college to which you are planning to transfer to see whether they will accept the credits from that institution.

If you are considering a clinical, technical, or professional program, make sure it is accredited by the professional accreditation agency in its respective discipline, such as the Accreditation Board for Engineering and Technology (ABET) for engineering programs or the Commission on Massage Therapy

Accreditation (COMTA) for massage therapy programs. To obtain a list of regional and national institutional accrediting agencies, visit www.ed.gov/ accreditation. Employers will usually give preference to students who graduate from accredited programs.

THE ADMISSIONS PROCESS

Although admissions standards vary from college to college, all of them will require a high school diploma or GED. In addition, many private and public universities and colleges have *selective* admissions standards, which mean they are very choosey about whom they accept. Private schools will require SAT or ACT examinations, an essay, and letters of recommendations in addition to the standard application and fees. Many public or state-owned universities will require similar items for consideration and may have an admission cutoff date. Because of their lower cost, as compared with private colleges and universities, admission to public universities is becoming more competitive because of the increased numbers of students trying to attend. Community colleges are generally the least expensive because their funding comes from their local communities and their mission is to serve the local workforce needs of their community. Community colleges and technical schools generally do not require SAT or ACT scores, an essay, or recommendations. They operate under an "open" admissions policy, which means they will accept every applicant who applies, providing they have a high school diploma or a GED.

Many colleges offer special provisions for adult students coming back to school, such as substituting placement examinations for high school grades or SAT scores or "forgiving" a previously earned grade point average after a certain number of years have passed since you last attended school. If you are transferring courses from another school, the good news is that only the credits transfer, not the grades. Classes with a grade of "C" or better are eligible to transfer. Many colleges require transfer students to have at least a 2.0 minimum grade point average for acceptance.

A COLLEGE CHECKLIST

1. Research colleges (on the web) to find a college that offers the major you're interested in.
2. Meet with that college's admissions personnel to obtain an application, learn about application requirements and procedures such as applications (paper format or on the web), application fees, whether they require an essay or SAT scores, and any special admissions

requirements for your particular major. Discuss what the college has to offer academically and nonacademically, take a tour, talk with faculty, and visit the academic department. If you have transfer credits from another institution, inquire about their transferability. Usually, core curriculum courses like English, history, math, social sciences, and general science will transfer. Technical courses in computer science, allied health, sciences, and engineering are usually considered outdated after several years and may have to be upgraded.

3. Apply for admission at least six months in advance. Every college has its own admissions requirements. Some have an application deadline, whereas others take students on a rolling basis (which means they continue to accept students until a class is filled). Community colleges will usually continue to accept students up until the first day of classes. If admission to the college you plan to attend is selective, ask whether there is a wait list or other mechanism to be considered.

4. Contact your high school or any previously attended colleges and request they send an official copy of your academic transcript to the admissions office of the school you plan to attend. If the high school or college you previously attended was shut down, contact your state's higher education agency for assistance. States are required to keep academic records.

5. Meet with financial aid personnel to discuss paying for college, application forms, etc.

6. Apply for financial aid and scholarships. Complete the FAFSA application in the spring before the semester you wish to enroll. This means you want to have your taxes done early. Apply before the deadline so you are considered for all of the money you're eligible for.

7. Respond to or "accept" your offer of admission. Most colleges will mail you a formal acceptance letter outlining the steps to accept, reject, or delay your admission.

8. Take your placement test. Placement tests are not really tests but are designed to assess your academic skills in such areas as reading, writing, English, math, and science. This ensures that you're not given courses that are too hard or too easy.

9. Respond to all financial aid documents. You will receive several pieces of correspondence from the federal government, your state, and the college regarding your eligibility for and amounts of grants, loans, scholarships, and work study funds. Respond to each granting agency by the appropriate response date.

10. Attend academic orientations or student advising sessions. Most colleges will invite you to an academic orientation in which you will meet with an advisor who will help you select your classes. Some schools combine this session with a general student orientation.

11. Attend student orientation. This orientation will acquaint you with the college and its resources, which are all put in place to help you succeed. Many colleges provide time during orientation to do things like sign up for a student e-mail account, register your car for parking, make adjustments to your schedule, get a student ID card, visit the gym or fitness center, or get acquainted with other students. In addition, the college will usually sponsor a large picnic or lunch, which gives you a chance to meet the faculty, staff, and other students before you start school.

12. Buy your books. If you look early enough, you may find "used" books, which are considerably cheaper than the price of a brand new book. Just make sure the pages are not disfigured with highlighting or notes.

13. Get a copy of your schedule. Most schedules are mailed to you before classes start. If for some reason you don't receive yours, stop at the registrar's office before classes begin and ask for a copy. Review your class schedule. Check to make sure you are registered for the right classes. Most colleges will allow you to add or drop classes or make other adjustments to your schedule up to the first week or ten days of classes. Know where all of your classes are located, even if you have to take a walk around campus a few days before classes start. Being familiar with the layout of campus and knowing the location of your classes will make your first day of class considerably less stressful!

It is very important to read and respond promptly to all letters you receive from the college or the state and federal government. I can't stress this enough. More than one student has missed out on a financial aid award deadline by not opening their mail or not responding to or following the directions in the letter. If you are going to be away on vacation, arrange to have your mail forwarded or have a relative or neighbor open your mail and contact you if the need arises.

EDUCATIONAL DELIVERY OPTIONS

Many adults do not have the time to commute long distances to and from school each day. Many colleges offer courses at sites other than their main campus location. So, you may be able to take classes at a location closer to your home. Keep in mind that not all of the courses required for your program may be offered there, but it is a place to start.

For students who simply do not have the time to commute to college or attend classes in a traditional classroom format, colleges offer classes in a number of alternative formats such as distance education, online courses, telecourses, or hybrid options. Some colleges offer academic programs on an accelerated basis that allow students to complete programs in a shorter period of time. Classes may be held year round or on a ten-week cycle instead of the traditional fifteen-week cycle. Other classes may be held only once a week or on weekends.

Another option designed to shorten the time it takes to complete your degree is receiving college credit for life and work experience. Some colleges accept credits from CLEP and DANTES examinations or provide a mechanism to evaluate work or life experience through a portfolio review or challenge examinations. All of these options are subject to a college's particular policies, and there is usually a limit on the number of life experience credits that can be applied to a program. Make sure you inquire about these details ahead of time.

If you are interested in obtaining a teaching certification, all forty-eight states in the continental U.S. currently have alternative certification programs in place. Alternative routes to education are opening career doors for thousands of adult students who might never have fulfilled their teaching dreams otherwise. Each state has its own specific rules, examinations, and requirements for teacher certification. To find out about each state's specific offerings, visit www.Teach-Now.org, The National Center for Alternative Certification's website.

HOW LONG WILL IT TAKE TO EARN MY DEGREE?

This is the question that's on every adult learner's mind. Because time is money and most adults have little of each, it pays to be able to complete your degree as quickly as possible.

The traditional academic year is divided into a fall (August or September to December) semester and a spring (January to May) semester. Some colleges offer an intersession, and some still run trimesters, or three semesters a year. All colleges offer classes in the summer, usually on a shortened basis. Most traditional semesters run fourteen or fifteen weeks. A full-time credit load is at least twelve credits (up to 18), and part-time enrollment is at least six credits. Because most associate degree programs require sixty-eight to seventy-two credits to graduate, it generally takes two years to complete a program. A baccalaureate program may require 120 to 140 credits to graduate, in about four years. If you attend part time, you can expect to double the time it takes to earn your degree.

The good news is that you will not be in school every day of the week as you were in high school. A class generally meets one hour for each credit, so a three credit class would meet three times a week (e.g. Monday, Wednesday, Friday) for fifty to sixty minutes, or two times a week (Tuesday and Thursday) for seventy-five minutes. Labs may meet for a two- to four-hour period of time once a week. If you attend classes at night, they will usually meet once a week for a three-hour period (6:00–9:00 PM). So if you schedule early enough, you may be able to construct a schedule that will allow for time to work or take care of family responsibilities.

The length of time needed to earn your degree may be extended if you need to take a remedial or refresher course in math, English, reading, or science. Taking refresher courses will be determined by your scores on your placement tests before scheduling classes. Students who need to take refresher courses are academically weak in a subject because they haven't been in school for years and are a bit "rusty" or did not take college preparatory courses in high school and simply do not have the prerequisite background needed for introductory college courses. Taking refresher courses may slow your progress down by a semester, but you won't succeed without taking them. Many students "place" into refresher courses and go on to be academically successful in their chosen program.

MAJORS AND MINORS

As discussed before, some college majors are designed to prepare you for a specific career. A major in accounting, for example, prepares students to be accountants, and an elementary education major prepares students to become K–6 teachers. Other majors, like English, history, communications, or philosophy, provide students with a broad-based education, a set of skills in critical thinking, writing and speaking, research, and an appreciation for cultural diversity that can be applied to almost any position in the work world.

Combining degree programs can make you more marketable. Some experts call this *dual* or *multicareer* planning. Employers in retail or insurance sales look favorably upon applicants who have degrees in psychology as well as business. A minor in Spanish, combined with a major degree in business administration, hotel and restaurant management, legal assisting, or health care, can make you very marketable in many parts of the country today.

Examples of new occupations that are really combinations of several majors are forensic accounting, health care law, biostatistics, and cyber security. While you are going to school, it is wise to be aware of new employment areas and trends. Remember that, ten years ago, we didn't know who a "webmaster" was or what someone in "e-commerce" did.

HOW TO BE SUCCESSFUL IN COLLEGE

The biggest mistakes made by college students are:

- Not reading or following directions.
- Not knowing deadlines for adding or dropping classes, withdrawing, applying for scholarships, etc.
- Not asking for help when they need it or waiting too long to get help.
- Not taking advantage of resources at the college.
- Poor time management.

Here's how to have a successful college career:

- Go to class. This is very important. Points may be added or deducted from your grade for attendance, and you may miss valuable information. Not going to class is one of the primary reasons why students do not do as well in a class as they should.
- Read your textbook. This material is assigned for a reason. Students who don't read (or even buy) their textbook do not do as well on examinations as other students because they miss valuable information that may be on the exam.
- Read and understand the syllabus. Consider the syllabus a contract between you and your teacher that outlines the professor's expectations and what you need to do to earn a particular grade in the class. Know when the due dates are for each quiz, project, examination, and homework assignment.
- Learn how to take good notes. You don't have to write down everything your professor says, just the main points. After class, recopy your notes and fill in the blank spots. Compare notes with classmates. Sometimes, they may hear something you missed and vice versa.
- Know what your grades are. Receiving a poor grade in a class should never be a surprise. Understand the grading system. Know what percentage of your grade is based on in-class discussion, quizzes, tests, projects, and extra credit. If you don't understand the grading system, ask the professor to explain it to you.

- Get a tutor, or enroll in a study session, if you find yourself starting to fall behind or do not perform as well as you would have liked on your first examination. Don't wait until the end of the semester to sign up for a tutor to try to bring up your grade because by then it is too late.

- Manage your time. Allow two to three hours of study time for every hour spent in class. Things are incredibly more accelerated at the college level. Study with a buddy or organize a small study group with a couple of classmates. It's like exercising; doing it with a friend will increase your chances of sticking with it.

- See your advisor at least once a semester to review your progress, preregister for the following semester, and to make sure you're taking the proper classes. Many students think they can do better on their own or consult their friends, only to find out they're missing a requirement. Your academic advisor knows the specific requirements of your program better than you or your friends do. Even if you do make a mistake in scheduling classes, your advisor may still be able to rectify the situation or suggest an alternative solution.

- If something unexpected comes up and you miss a class (e.g., you or your children are sick, you have an appointment that can't be scheduled any other time, someone in your family has an emergency, etc.), tell your professor. Informing your professor ahead of time will show that you are committed to the class, responsible, and didn't just blow it off. Many professors, depending on their classroom policy, will give students a number of allowable class "cuts" or allow you to make up an assignment. Get the missed lecture notes from a classmate. If you are in a situation where you're going to be out of school for more than a week, tell your academic advisor as well as your professor. Sometimes, students have to take an "incomplete" grade in one or more classes and finish the requirements the following semester or take a medical withdrawal and reenroll the next semester. Withdrawing saves your grade point average.

- Never stop attending classes without first talking with someone, no matter how hopeless, awful, stupid, or embarrassing you think your situation is. (There isn't anything you can tell your counselor or academic advisor that they haven't heard before). If you stop attending class or drop out of school without completing formal withdrawal forms, you will earn Fs in all of your classes. The college doesn't know what happened to you, and because you are an adult, they will not withdraw you from school without prior written authorization. You really do not want to end up with all Fs on your academic record because this is something that will haunt you the rest of your life and jeopardize your future educational and financial aid status.

- Take charge of your learning (just like when looking for a job). Don't rely on teachers to teach you, you must learn the material. Ask if you don't understand something the professor discussed in class. Most professors have office hours during which students can come in and ask questions.
- Sit in front of the class so you don't miss anything and allow the teacher to get to know you. You are paying a lot of money for your education, so get the most out of it!
- If you have little work experience, get involved in extracurricular activities so you have something to put on your resume. Leadership experience, initiative, and working with people are all traits employers are looking for.

Chapter 10

Reenter the Workforce

When one door closes another door opens; but we so often look so long and so regretfully upon the closed door, that we do not see the ones which open for us.

Alexander Graham Bell

Whether you have decided to find another job or go back to school, the end result is that you will need to look for a new job. If you have not searched for a job in a while, you will notice that there have been some changes in the way we apply for jobs as well as in the workplace itself. The job market is much more competitive than it used to be, and some of the old methods simply no longer apply. You may need to create a resume or a portfolio for the first time in your career or submit your resume online instead of mailing it in.

To help you make the most of your job search efforts and avoid making common job seeking mistakes, this chapter will focus on using your skills and assets to develop an effective resume and cover letter, identify places to apply to or potential employers to contact, and some tips for the interviewing process.

RESUME HIGHLIGHTS

There are many good books out there that cover resume writing and interviewing skills in great detail. The purpose of this chapter is not to duplicate the information in those books but to emphasize the key items that will increase your chances of being selected for an interview.

Use a Career Summary

To be successful in your job search in today's competitive job market, your resume and cover letter must be action-driven and clearly demonstrate the value you bring to a company. Summarize your main accomplishments and job responsibilities by using a *Career Summary* or *Profile* at the top of your resume instead of an *Objective*. The problem with using an *Objective* is that they are often too specific, too broad, or tend to convey an "I" centered approach rather than an "employer centered" approach. A well-written *Career Summary* is much more effective in capturing an employer's attention and conveying your value to their organization. Remember, you want to make it as easy as possible for the interviewer to come to the conclusion that you are the most qualified candidate for the job.

Match Your Skills to the Requirements of the Job

When applying for a position, pay close attention to what is written in the job description. Your resume and cover letter should match the skills and experience required by a particular job. For example, if a position requires a strong *organizational ability,* give specific examples of your organizational skills such as "Able to prioritize projects and complete tasks for eight professionals in a busy sales office;" "Able to gather data and generate reports within a twenty-four-hour period of time."

Use Action-Oriented Verbs

Instead of writing "Excellent computer skills," be more specific by saying "Proficient in Microsoft Word, Excel, and PowerPoint." And remember to start each sentence with an action-oriented verb such as *achieved, assembled, assisted, coordinated, evaluated, improved, managed, performed, produced, researched, sold, supervised, trained.* Avoid phrases such as "responsible for" or "duties included," which can create a passive tone. Instead, use active verbs to describe what you actually did such as "Wrote and designed flyers and brochures for new products" or "Developed a new sales brochure."

Keywords

Today, many large companies use applicant-tracking software to match resumes with open positions via *keywords.* Keywords and keyword phrases are terminology or jargon specific to your profession (usually nouns). Examples of occupational specific keywords are "Microsoft Office proficient," "AutoCAD 2008," "Chair side dental assisting," or "Team oriented." Use keywords to highlight your accomplishments in the *Summary, Skills,* or *Employment* sections of your resume. If a company is seeking a candidate with specific skills or qualifications, the applicant-tracking software will automatically select all of the resumes that include those words or phrases. You don't want to be passed over because you do not have the "right" words in your resume.

Gaps in Your Employment History

If you have been out of the workforce for a long time, you may be wondering how to handle any gaps in your employment history. Generally, employers like to see a pattern of job stability and progression within your career. The best advice is to address an employer's potential concerns right up front in the cover letter. Indicate that you interrupted your career to raise your children but that now you are in a position to resume your career. When listing previous positions, eliminate those held on a temporary or short-term (under a year) basis or those held more than fifteen years ago. The only exception is if the duties in a particular position were directly related to the position you are applying for today. If your situation is such that you don't have a lot of employment history but held a volunteer position for a school, health care facility, or nonprofit agency, go ahead and list those positions but specifically identify them as "volunteer" experience.

Changing Careers

If you are changing careers, one strategy is to pull out relevant skills, experience, and accomplishments (remember the exercises in Chapter 4?) from previous positions and highlight them under a special heading (or group of headings) at the top of your resume. You can then list all of your *Customer Service* experience and skills in one paragraph, and your *Management* or *Web Development* skills in another.

If your previous position was secretarial or clerical in nature and you want to apply for a job in sales, then emphasize your former customer service and communication skills rather than your accounts payable or computer skills. The trick is to convert, or adapt, your previous work experience to support what will be required in your new job. If you are not sure how to do this, try this strategy: on a sheet of paper, list everything you did in your old job on a daily basis, then pull out those duties or skills that can be used to support what is required in the new position. For example, here's a job description for a sales associate:

Seeking an accounts manager for a local Internet provider. Duties include servicing existing customer accounts and cultivating new customers, informing customers of new products or services, and responding to customers' questions and concerns. Must be organized, computer literate, and able to deliver high-quality customer service.

From the job description, you can see that this position requires good communication, organizational, and customer service skills. Let's assume for a moment that your previous position was as a secretary for an electronics store. After reviewing the daily responsibilities of your former secretarial position, you could pull out the following relevant job responsibilities:

- "Daily interaction with customers of all ages and backgrounds" (interpersonal communication).
- "First line contact for customer inquiries. Able to calmly respond to customer concerns and direct their inquiries to the appropriate service department" (interpersonal communication and customer service).
- "Able to prioritize multiple projects from several supervisors and complete projects within deadline" (organizational abilities).

If you worked in a business office, you might be able to say, "Quickly identified the source of customers' dissatisfaction and worked to resolve the issue to the customers' satisfaction." If your job was to describe products or services over the phone in response to customer inquiries, you could write, "Clearly and concisely described products and services to existing customers, identified customers' needs, and appropriately suggested services or products." The latter is directly applicable to the sales world.

The Issue of Age

If you do not have a lot of work experience because you are just beginning your career or you have been out of the workforce for some time, capitalize on the skills and experiences you do have to date. Activities to draw from are any volunteer work you did with your local school, church, library, or other civic group. Maybe you watched your neighbor's children during the day, or took classes at night, or "unofficially" acted as secretary and bookkeeper for your husband's business, all of which can be claimed as work experience.

On the other hand, if you have the opposite situation (too much experience) or are worried about showing your age, use a resume format that emphasizes your skills and experience by beginning the resume with a *Career Summary* (also called a *Profile, Summary of Highlights*, or *Summary of Qualifications*). A *Career Summary* gives you the opportunity to position yourself as you want to be perceived. The other nice feature about using a *Career*

Summary is that you can include all the skills and experience you acquired over the years through both paid work experiences and unpaid volunteer experiences.

To deemphasize dates, place them on the right-hand side of your resume under the *Work Experience* section instead of on the left-hand side of the resume as you would when using a chronological resume style. Another strategy is to omit dates altogether and list number of years worked instead. If you are still employed at a position, include the word "current" after the number of years. Here's an example from a *Work Experience* section of a resume:

Farm Bureau Credit Union, Columbus, Ohio   4 years (current)
Senior Accountant
   • Prepare payroll, tax returns, and various reports and tax forms.
Self-Employed, Columbus, Ohio   2 years
Certified Public Accountant
   • Prepared individual tax forms and returns for clients.

Electronic Resumes

If you plan to post your resume online, be aware that most commercial Internet resume-posting or job search databases are organized by occupational categories (keywords). This allows employers to search for relevant resumes rather than wasting time reviewing resumes of individuals without the proper qualifications. Design your resume with the goal of increasing the number of matches between what an employer is looking for in a candidate and your resume. Many large commercial databases like Career-Builder.com organize their searches by specific categories such as skills, experience, and education. When asked to submit your resume, type it in plain text format. Even though some databases are able to upload a resume prepared in a Word document, they will still convert it to a plain text file for posting.

The design of an electronic resume is different than a traditional paper-and-pencil format. Include relevant keywords in a separate section or in your summary. These are the words employers will use to select relevant resumes from the database. The main difference is that the plain text resume is devoid of fancy fonts, typesets, graphics, or shading. Another difference is that skill-focused nouns, such as *management, counselor,* or *writer,* or keywords are used throughout the text rather than action-oriented verbs.

Here's a rundown of the differences between traditional and electronic resumes.

Traditional Resume	Electronic Resume
Mailed to an employer	E-mailed or posted to a website
Written in any format	Written in ASCII or plain text format
Use any type of typeface or font	Use a standard type face and 12 point font
Left- or center-justified format	Left-justified format
Use any sentence length	Do not exceed 65 characters in a sentence
Uses wrap-around feature or page breaks	End each sentence with a hard return
Use any format for name, address, phone	Write name and address on separate lines
Use action verbs	Use skill-based nouns
Use any font to emphasize headers	Capitalize letters to emphasize headers
Use bullets to outline	Use an asterisk, dash, or plus sign
Can use special fonts or effects	Do not use bold, italics, underline, shading, graphics, parenthesis, horizontal lines
Conversational style job descriptions	Contains keywords depicting skills, education, accomplishments, and experience
Printed on light colored or white paper	E-mailed or uploaded from a computer file

COVER LETTERS

A cover letter introduces you to the employer and gives the reader a taste of what is to be found in the resume. It should be professional, yet friendly, and convey competence and congeniality. The cover letter should be short and to the point; summarizing key experience, skills, or accomplishments and always referring the reader to your resume.

In today's economy, there are more applicants for jobs than there are openings. The best applicant for the job is the one whose skills and experience most closely fit the needs of the company. It helps to try to view your credentials from the perspective of an employer. When crafting your cover letter and resume, ask yourself how your skills and knowledge can best help the company, rather than what you're going to get out of the job. Viewing the process from the employer's eyes will make all the difference. Employers will naturally throw up a red flag at a resume from someone who has hasn't worked for several years, has too little or too much work experience for the position, has a sporadic employment history, or is drastically changing careers. The human tendency is to wonder what the real story behind a person's desire to leave his or her job is. My advice is to address these unspoken concerns right up front in the cover letter.

Employers are acutely aware of company closures in the area. Stating that you are seeking a new position because of a recent company closure is an acceptable and blameless reason for seeking a new position. Likewise, address the issue of gaps in your employment history by stating that, after raising your children (or caring for an ill parent), you are now ready to continue your career.

Regarding the issue of salary (especially for those of you who were laid off from a high-paying management-level position), you want to assure the employer that you are willing to accept a lower salary than you previously enjoyed or that you realize you are entering a new career, which may include beginning at an entry-level salary. Remember, the purpose of the resume (and accompanying cover letter) is to entice an employer to invite you in for an interview. Address these issues *before* the employer has a chance to formulate his or her opinion or speculation. Failure to do so may preclude you from being invited in for an interview where you could fully explain your situation and circumstances.

THE PROCESS OF LOOKING FOR A JOB

There are two ways to psychologically approach the issue of finding a job. One way is from the perspective of what the job has to offer you personally and professionally, and the second is what the employer can gain from your skills and experience. Both are important. Your personal preferences determine how happy and satisfied you are going to be on the job. The second determines your "hireability," or the degree to which an employer will want your skills and experience.

Many career strategists have said that searching for a job *is* a full-time job. This cannot be emphasized enough, especially in today's tight job market. You must spend a block of time each day searching for job openings. Also, too many people miss out on possible job opportunities because they make assumptions about a position without gathering the facts. They assume the job is not something they'd want or that the employer will not be interested in them. If you are a single mother having difficulty finding a full-time position because of childcare issues, continue to apply for all open positions, even those that specify hours that would potentially conflict with childcare, because circumstances often change. I worked with a young mother who could not work beyond 5:00 PM because of childcare issues. When an ideal position opened up near her home, she did not apply for the position because the ad listed the work hours from 9 to 6. However, as it turned out, the employer was unable to fill the position and later told me that he was so desperate that he would have been willing to accommodate her needs. By not applying for the position, she automatically ruled out any possibility of being able to discuss, or negotiate, the situation during the interview.

Throughout your job search, you must continue to package and promote your skills to the right employers. Chapter 4 introduced the concept of your "employability package." Your employability package is the job market package you are attempting to sell to a potential employer. It not only consists of your education, experience, skills, accomplishments, and areas of expertise but also your personal characteristics, your enthusiasm, ability to get along with others, work ethic, and whether you are calm, creative, analytical, or spontaneous. The latter is much more subjective but nonetheless plays an important role in the hiring decision. At the end of every interview, an employer basically wants to know three things: a) CAN you do the job, b) WILL you do the job, and c) are you going to GET ALONG with the rest of the staff.

INTERVIEWING TIPS

To increase your chances of being hired, follow these eight basic steps:

1. **Research the company.** Before you walk into the interview, try to find out as much as possible about the company. An employer will be impressed that you took the time to research the company. Knowing a few things about an employer will also help you decide whether the company is right for you.

2. **Bring your resume.** Bring along an extra copy of your resume as well as a portfolio, if appropriate. Don't assume that everyone who is interviewing you has thoroughly read your resume. Know your resume like the back of your hand. If you incorrectly answer a question based on your resume, you will lose all credibility with the employer.

3. **Practice answering interview questions.** Practice so you can answer questions directly and honestly. Try to provide concrete examples of situations where you took the initiative, completed something as part of a team, solved a problem, or went above and beyond the call of duty.

4. **Be ready to ask questions.** The interview is about getting, as well as giving, information. Asking the interviewer questions not only demonstrates that you have a genuine interest in the company but helps you determine whether this is a company you want to work for. Ask the interviewer to describe the position and duties, explain why the position is vacant, describe the corporate philosophy or the supervisor's management style, describe what a typical day would be like, and what they expect from an employee. However, this is NOT the time to ask about salary or benefits.

5. **Know exactly where the interview takes place.** Drive by the company a day before the interview and make a note of how long it took you to get there. Plan to arrive at least ten minutes early and never, ever, show up even one minute late.

6. **Make a good impression.** You never get a second chance to make a first impression. Dress in appropriate business attire, smile, offer a firm handshake, and make good eye contact with the interviewer. Be polite, courteous, and look alert at all times. Remember, you only have a short period of time to make a good impression.

7. **Thank the interviewer.** Always thank the interviewer for his or her time and consideration. If you are interested in the position, don't be afraid to let them know.

8. **Follow up the interview with a thank-you note.** This is a necessary courtesy. E-mail or write a short note thanking the interviewer for the opportunity to interview and once again remind the employer that you're still very interested in the position.

Twenty of the Most Commonly Asked Interview Questions

The following are questions you should prepare answers for in advance:

1. "Tell me about yourself."
2. "Why are you interested in working here?"
3. "Tell me about your work experience." Or, "How have your educational and work experiences prepared you for this position?"
4. "Which experiences have been the most valuable to you and why?"
5. "What are your strongest traits? Your weakest?"
6. "What has been your greatest challenge?"
7. "Describe a situation where you had a conflict with another individual and how you dealt with it."

8. "Describe your leadership style." (Appropriate for management positions.)

9. "In a particular leadership role you had, what was the greatest challenge?"

10. "Give me an example of an idea you developed that was creative or innovative."

11. "Give me an example of how you work with others."

12. "How do you deal with pressure/stress?"

13. "Tell me about a difficult decision you have made."

14. "Give me an example of a situation that was not successful and how you handled it."

15. "What can you contribute to this company/department?"

16. "What characteristics are most important in a good manager? How have you displayed these characteristics?" (Appropriate for management positions.)

17. "Are you willing to relocate or travel as part of your job?"

18. "Describe the accomplishment that has given you the most satisfaction."

19. "What are your future plans/goals?"

20. "Why should we hire you?"

Employers will often ask open-ended questions (like many of those above) in the interview. You, however, must answer succinctly and back up your statements with examples whenever possible (e.g., "I was able to improve our admissions procedure by streamlining several pieces of intake documentation."). Don't become sidetracked into telling stories or spending too much time on one aspect of a question and neglecting the rest of the question. When describing what you did or enjoyed at a previous position, think like an employer. Focus your answers on the job and job tasks you did at work, like the specific accounting software you used, not on how much you loved being close to home, or the size of your office, or the quality of the cafeteria.

Whenever possible, always try to approach the situation from the perspective of what you can do for the company and how you can be an asset to *them* rather than what they can or will do for you and your career. Hiring an employee is a business decision, and the position is only open because they have a particular need to fill. Your job is to convince them that *you* are the candidate that will best meet their needs.

Handling Tough Interview Questions

One of the messages you want to convey is that you are ready to work, even after an absence. Human nature being what it is, employers are naturally going to wonder whether you're qualified, why you *really* left your job, and what kind of employee you were. Employers are hesitant to invest time, money, training, and resources in a new employee only to have them leave after a few months for greener pastures. Therefore, you must address an employer's unspoken questions (the red flags) during the interview process. The following are some common "red flags" (spoken or unspoken employer questions) and examples of responses (assurances) to those questions.

Red Flag #1: "Why is this person looking for a new job?

Assurance: Explain that the reason you are searching for a new position is that you were laid off from your former company; you had the opportunity to return to school to retrain for a new career; or, after staying at home to raise your children, you are now in a position to resume your career.

Red Flag #2: "You will want too much money"

Assurance: Make it clear that you are not expecting to receive the same salary as you did at your last position, that you are willing to be flexible. Other possible responses are that you have decided to make a career change and realize you may need to start at an entry level position, or you are only seeking part-time employment and do not need benefits. If you previously were receiving a much higher salary than the job you are interviewing for now pays, try to convince the employer that you are willing to take a cut in pay because you prefer to return to your former profession. Outline the value-added benefits of hiring someone with your years of experience and what that experience will bring to the position and to the company. If you're in a situation where you do not need employee benefits, (i.e., you are covered under your spouse or partner's plan or took an early retirement), convey that to the employer and reiterate your sincere desire to return to the profession you love. You may even be able to negotiate a higher salary in lieu of employee benefits.

Red Flag #3: "You are out of date, it's been too long since you worked, you have gaps in your employment history, etc."

Assurance: Explain that although it has been some time since you worked in your field, you have upgraded your skills by attending (name of school, workshop, conference, licensing), you have kept up with the latest advances in your field (perhaps through volunteer work, home business, etc.), that, because you have been out of work, you are especially eager to resume your former position with little need for a refresher.

Red Flag #4: *"Why are you making a career change?"*

Assurance: Explain the reasons for your decision to change careers. Include something to the effect that this career was always something you wanted to do and that now you have the opportunity to pursue your passion. Emphasize any training you recently completed in preparation for your new career or any transferable skills gained from previous positions. If you are changing careers because you are no longer physically able to perform your past profession, acknowledge the fact but assure the employer that your physical injuries have been resolved and will not interfere with your new duties. For example, you may want to say, "Although I can no longer do heavy lifting because of my knees, this will not prevent me from performing my duties as an accounting clerk," or, "I was able to find a career I enjoyed that does not aggravate my injury."

Red Flag #5: *"What have you been doing since your last job?"*

Assurance: Explain that you made the decision to stay home and raise your family or were caring for a sick family member, but now your children have graduated and you are now ready to go back to work. If you were laid off and were unable to find work, state that you took the opportunity to go back to school, did volunteer work, or worked from home or on a part-time basis while continuing to look for work in your field, or took the time to reflect on what you wanted to do next with your career. If you were recuperating from an injury or disability, illustrate your motivation and determination to prepare yourself for the workplace. Provide specific examples of how you spent your recuperative time through keeping up to date in your field, taking classes, volunteering in your community, or working part time at a related position.

Red Flag #6: *"You have too much education or work experience"*

Assurance: Acknowledge that you do have more experience than what is required but explain the advantages, benefits, and expertise that you can bring to the company. The real issue behind this red flag is that the potential employer will think that you will leave as soon as another position comes along. Do your best to assure him or her that this is not the case and that you are genuinely interested in working for the company or doing that particular line of work.

Red Flag #7: *"You have too little work experience"*

Assurance: If you don't have enough work experience because you recently graduated from college, highlight any outstanding accomplishments in school, job-related experiences through internship or volunteer work, or anything else that shows maturity or leadership ability. If you have limited work experience because you interrupted your career to raise a family, acknowledge that fact but explain that you have kept your skills up to date and can bring a level of maturity and stability to the position because of your life experience. In either case, make sure you illustrate how you believe you can do the job despite your perceived lack of work experience.

Red Flag #8: *"You do not have a degree, or your degree is in a different industry"*

Assurance: Emphasize your related skills, work experience, and accomplishments to offset your lack of formal education. Demonstrate your commitment to lifelong learning by highlighting any continuing education courses, workshops, or conferences you attended or your participation in work-sponsored training. If you are in the process of earning your degree or are considering going back to school, be sure to mention that to the employer.

I once interviewed a woman in her late fifties for a secretarial position in my office. Naturally, I wondered what prompted her to apply for this position (which paid much less than what she was previously making). She explained that she had retired early from her former employer to care for an ill family member. Now that her obligation was completed, she was looking to get back into the workforce again. Because she responded honestly and without hesitation, my concerns were alleviated, and she turned out to be a wonderful asset to our office.

Again, the employer is looking for any reasonable answer to their unspoken questions to ensure that you will be a good fit for the company.

Using a Portfolio in the Interview

Traditionally, portfolios have been used by artists and writers to showcase their work to potential employers. Today, portfolios are being used by job seekers in many different fields such as education, graphic design, marketing, sales, engineering, communications, public relations, information technology, and health sciences.

A portfolio is a collection of your work documenting your experiences and activities, training and preparation, and skills and accomplishments. A portfolio is best used as a "show and tell" tool to provide supporting evidence of your skills and abilities during a job interview. Portfolios are especially useful for people who have a lot of unpaid or volunteer experience as a way to showcase or demonstrate their achievements and skills in lieu of formal paid work experience. A good portfolio can also negate concerns of age or lack of experience because the proof of your ability is right there in front of the prospective employer.

The portfolio can be housed in a three-ring binder, a folder, or an artist's leather portfolio. Use clear plastic sleeves to protect your materials. A good size is approximately ten to twenty pages. You may want to consider a digital or electronic version of your portfolio. You could put your portfolio on the web, bring a stand-alone version on a laptop to the interview, or produce it all on a CD, which you could leave with the employer. If you really want to impress a potential employer, you can showcase your skills by adding sound bites, video clips, and animation. Reference your portfolio at the bottom of your resume with a statement such as "Portfolio Available for Review," or "Portfolio Available at www ... ."

What to include in your portfolio is going to depend on your career field. A graphic artist would have samples of flyers, brochures, or web pages. A teacher would have lesson plans, evaluation forms, and samples of curricula, classroom projects, and activities. An interior decorator would include pictures of completed rooms, measured drawings, and customer recommendations. A basic portfolio should include the following:

1. A copy of your resume.

2. Educational or training credentials: diplomas, CEU certificates, transcripts.

3. Work samples: writing samples, research papers, projects, designs, drawings, publications, proposals, flyers, web pages, grant proposals, workshop presentations, and photographs of large pieces of work.

4. Any commendations or awards: press releases, thank-you notes from clients, performance reviews, newspaper clippings, award notifications.

5. Professional memberships: membership certification, documentation of participation.

6. Community involvement: volunteer activities, sports teams, religious or civic activities, participation on committees or in community events.

When presenting your portfolio to a prospective employer, only include those items needed to apply for that particular position. Reorganize and edit your portfolio to suit each position and company. Sometimes, it's useful to review the job description and use that as a guide to select examples that will demonstrate how your skills and achievements meet the requirements of the job.

When using a portfolio in the interview, don't hand it to the employer at the beginning of the interview or save it until the end. Use the portfolio to provide examples of your skills and accomplishments in response to interview questions. This means that your portfolio should be well organized so you can find your materials as quickly and smoothly as possible.

WHERE TO SEARCH FOR JOB OPENINGS

In today's tight job market, you need to take an active role in finding an employer. Don't just rely on advertisements in the Sunday newspaper; use networking, Internet job search sites, and cold-calling techniques.

Many career experts recommend using the "hidden job market" to find positions. The "hidden job market" consists of job openings that that have not been advertised publicly. When an employee turns in their resignation, the person in charge of hiring begins the process of looking through old resumes and asking colleagues for recommendations. If a suitable candidate is found, then there is no need to take the search to the next level and place an ad in the newspaper. Hence, the job opening was filled before most people knew it was open. As a job seeker, the trick is to be in the right place at the right time before the job is opened to the general public. How do you make that happen? Through networking, cold-calling techniques, and making inquiries at companies you would like to work for.

Although many jobs are filled in-house or through word-of-mouth referrals, many are not. A job seeker's success in finding a position in the hidden job market depends on the type of job you are looking for and the typical hiring practices of your particular industry or occupation. For example, at the college where I work, *all* jobs are advertised in the newspaper, and a formal selection process is followed. Nurses, on the other hand, because of the high demand in our area, need only connect with a nursing recruiter at a job fair or fill out an application to receive multiple offers. However, there are many small businesses in my area that prefer to rely on word-of-mouth advertising because it is less expensive than placing a formal ad in the newspaper and less time-consuming than interviewing dozens of applicants who may or may not be qualified for the position.

Less than ten years ago, it was common practice to blindly mail out hundreds of generic cover letters and resumes to a list of potential companies and wait for a response. Often, the response rate was pretty dismal, although those who received job offers through that method could argue that the method was successful. In any case, today, unsolicited resumes are viewed as junk mail. Instead, I recommend looking through the phone book or surfing the Internet to identify a few potential companies and then either call or e-mail a human resource manager and inquire about any future openings. This method not only saves money on stamps but involves less time waiting for a response. If a company is interested, they will ask you to send a resume. If they are not interested, then you will know that up front and won't waste your time waiting for a response that may never come. If asked to submit a resume, the key to success with this method is to follow up by phone or e-mail two weeks later and then continue to keep in touch every four to six weeks until someone has been hired or the position is no longer open.

Internet Job Searching

The Internet is very helpful if you are looking for a job in a large industry (business, sales, health care, engineering, technology) or if you are looking for a job in a different part of the country. Internet job searching is most useful if you know exactly what field or type of industry you are searching for. Internet search engines use databases to allow employers (and job seekers) to quickly and efficiently identify a pool of candidates that best match a particular job opening. Matching is based on keywords. Because job seekers have to enter their educational and employment information within predetermined categories, there is less opportunity or flexibility to emphasize, omit, or creatively group skills and experience as there is when using an electronic or paper resume. Therefore, Internet job searching is going to be less effective for job seekers who do not have a specific employment goal or occupation in mind. If you are trying to change careers, it is very important to emphasize the keywords that directly relate to your current career plans. There are a number of ways to do this, namely, sprinkling them in the *Summary*, *Objective*, and *Job Description* sections of your resume and wherever appropriate in the application itself.

How Big Is Your Network?

Don't underestimate the power of networking. Think of networking as having twenty friends helping you find a job. Word-of mouths referrals are very effective because (1) you *know* there's a legitimate job opening, (2) you will be aware of more job openings using this method; in other words, openings that you may never have been aware of because you weren't looking at that particular newspaper or weren't privy to a certain conversation or in a particular meeting where it was discussed, and (3) you have an advantage over other candidates by being personally recommended for the position by someone who has an "in" with the company.

Here are some possible networking sources:

- Current or old business contacts.
- Previous customers or clients.
- People in any professional organizations you may belong to.
- Individuals you know socially or through a community organization such as your aerobics class, your son or daughter's soccer team, or members on a recycling committee.
- Friends, relatives, neighbors.
- Professional or community contacts like your accountant, gardener, veterinarian, or physician.

Cumulatively, these people have the potential of talking to hundreds of unrelated individuals each week, many more than you could ever hope to talk to in the normal course of your day! So ask anyone you meet (within reason, of course) to keep you in mind if they should hear of an opening. You never know whose paths will cross in the future.

To increase the chances of successfully finding a job, use multiple resources rather than a single method or source of openings. If you are looking for a job in a market that has lots of openings, you may only need to use one source to find employment. But if you live in an economically depressed area where there have been many layoffs, you will probably have to use all of the resources at your disposal to find a job. Don't be afraid to check trade journals, occupational specific websites, or even visit an executive recruiter or staffing agency.

Additional Job Search Sources

Here are a few other places to find job leads:

1. Public employment services such as your One-Stop Career Center, your local chamber of commerce, and community job posting sites.
2. Internet job boards, job search engines, company websites, and websites for specific industries or professional organizations.

3. College or university career offices and alumni organizations.

4. Women's centers and community-based career services for people who belong to a particular "special populations" category, such as single parents, displaced homemakers, or members of an underrepresented group based on gender or ethnicity.

5. Trade magazines, professional organizations, and industry or occupational specific Internet sites and job boards.

6. Job or career fairs in your local or regional area.

7. Executive recruiters or employment agencies (also called staffing or personnel agencies). When using these agencies, find out whether they charge you, or the employer, a fee for their services.

A Realistic Word about Salaries

You need to be keenly aware of the market value of your skills. Most companies want to hire and retain the most qualified people for the job, but not every company is willing to spend the same amount for an employee. Some employers are willing to pay more for qualified workers, although most employers will tend to base their salary scales on the average salary rates in their geographic area.

If you are planning to look for a job within the same career field, you will be making a lateral or upward move, which in most cases will allow you to retain a similar, or preferably higher, salary than you are currently making. However, if you are making a dramatic career change to a different industry (such as a production worker making a career change to the accounting field), you may have to begin your new career at an entry-level position. Unfortunately, this means you'll be starting at, or just above, the entry-level salary for that occupation. The good news is that experienced employees in entry-level positions are sometimes able to start at a higher salary because of their cumulative work experience and are promoted at a faster rate than entry-level employees without experience. But this varies by company and industry. An entry-level salary in nursing, for example, may be higher than some mid-level management positions, so do your research beforehand and know what salary to expect for your geographic area.

If you haven't been able to find work or know you will be starting in a new career at a lower salary, you want to disarm an employer's natural tendency to jump to the conclusion that you're going to be "too expensive." Therefore, you need to make it very clear up front that you are fully aware that you are making a career change and may have to start at an entry-level salary or that you are comfortable starting at a salary commensurate with your experience in your new field (in other words, a lower salary). If you have been laid off and are applying for a position in your field that is considerably lower than what you used to make, try to convey how much you enjoyed being in your profession (or doing the work that you love), and, at this point in your life, it is more important to get back into your field than regain your salary.

Employers don't want to waste anyone's time, especially their own, interviewing candidates who aren't really interested in the position once they hear what the salary is. Likewise, they have no desire to invest time and training in candidates only to watch them leave as soon as they find a better position. Addressing this concern up front may prevent an employer from automatically assuming you would not be interested or would be too expensive and tossing your resume in the trash bin.

After the Interview

Waiting for an employer to offer you the job is the hardest part of the interview process. You may have walked out of the interview feeling great; you answered all the questions correctly, received enthusiastic responses from interviewers, felt the chemistry was right, yet you still haven't heard anything from them. But remember that *their* time is not your time. While you are anxiously waiting for a call, they may have to present your resume to their board, or wait for the decision maker to return from vacation, or have to deal with some last minute budget readjustments that may delay matters. If the organization is a government or educational institution, the selection process may be extremely slow and cumbersome because of all the levels of administration the application needs to go through for approval to hire someone for a position. All of these factors are internal to the employer and have nothing to do with you. Try to keep this in mind while you wait.

If you are really interested in the position, send a brief handwritten thank-you note to the interviewer. This is a technique that is rarely used but is effective and appreciated. Thank the interviewer for the opportunity to speak with them, highlight any experience or qualifications you feel are relevant, and reiterate your interest in the position. Unfortunately, in today's busy age, you may not even get a response that your application was received unless you are one of the few selected to come in for an interview. You should, however, be diligent about following up every two to four weeks while you continue to look for new openings.

Whenever possible, try to identify the reasons why you *didn't* get a position so you will know what to do differently next time. Perhaps your resume needed to be written in a different way to highlight your skills and experience? Maybe you were over or under qualified? Was there a more qualified candidate in the application pool? Do you need to practice how you come across in an interview? How is your handshake? Did you use the appropriate amount of eye contact, answer the questions thoroughly, ask intelligent questions, and convey a professional image? Or did you mumble or ramble on in response to questions, slouch in your chair, chew gum, or use body language that suggested you would not be a good candidate? Practice makes perfect when interviewing, so learn from your mistakes and keep on interviewing. Eventually, you will find the right match and be offered the job!

Chapter 11

Afterword: Where Do I Go from Here?

Success is not a destination; it is a journey.

Zig Ziglar

A job can be a source of satisfaction or a source of misery. The good news is that you can choose which kind of situation to have. Most of you will be following two basic formulas for improving your employment situation.

The formula for finding a new job:

- Write a resume or update an existing one
- Identify possible employers and companies
- Actively search for job openings
- Apply, interview, wait, and repeat the process until you get a job offer

The formula for upgrading your skills to find a better job:

- Go back to school
- Graduate
- Update your resume
- Identify possible employers and companies and search for job openings
- Apply, interview, wait, and repeat the process until you get a job offer

FINDING WORK THAT YOU ENJOY

We all want to do work that makes us feel good about ourselves, and we all want to be in a position where we can be successful and make a positive contribution. When you love what you're doing, you are using your talents to their best advantage. Spending your time doing what makes you happy is what creates a fulfilled and satisfied life.

In my experience, people who have been successful in creating a more satisfying employment situation share the following traits:

- They are proactive in their job search. They actively seek out openings rather than waiting for jobs to come to them.
- They find a way to pursue their dreams by overcoming their obstacles, fears, and "yes, buts."
- They take the necessary steps to improve their employability by improving their educational background, learning new skills, or improving their job search strategy or interviewing presentation.
- They feel their careers are in their control rather than outside of their control or in the hands of fate.
- They are able to find an interest, develop a goal, make a plan, and persist despite challenges.

THE DECISION TO GO BACK TO SCHOOL OR GO BACK INTO THE WORKFORCE

If you are recently unemployed or are forced to find a new job or career, hopefully you have taken the time to reflect on your life and think about what you'd like to do in the future. If you were able to make a decision about which direction to take your future, was your decision based on the following factors?

1. Did you identify your interests, work values, transferable skills, strengths, and weaknesses?
2. Did you compare what you have (skills, work experience, education) with what is needed in your career in today's workplace?
3. Did you identify the areas that needed to be improved?
4. If you needed help in deciding on a career, did you take an interest inventory or talk with a career counseling professional?

5. Did you carefully research your chosen career, industry, or employer?

6. Did you thoughtfully weigh both positive and negative costs, consequences, and outcomes of each decision?

7. Were you able to generate solutions to what you once believed were barriers that stopped you from pursuing your career?

8. Did you explore all of the options available to you (such as moving to a different job within your organization, finding a new job or a new employer, or going back to school to train for a new career or upgrade an outdated credential?)

9. Have you made detailed plans to implement your career choice, gotten the required education, and marketed yourself and searched for a job?

If you can honestly answer "yes" to these questions, you can be reasonably assured that you have made a good decision. Congratulate yourself. You have made a tremendous step forward in your life. Now, it's time to move forward with that decision. Some steps can be acted upon quite quickly (like drafting a resume and applying for openings). Others, like going back to school, require a little more patience before you act and then see the desired outcome.

Remember the young man working in a warehouse who wanted to be a CPA? He didn't have to give up his dream of becoming a CPA, he just had to delay it for a while. Taking a few key courses in accounting allowed him to find an entry-level position in the career field he enjoyed. Even though this position wasn't at the level at which he wanted to be, it was much more palatable than staying at his warehousing job. He still had the option of continuing on for a four-year degree or eventual CPA certification by going to school at night. The advantage of holding a steady job with benefits during the day with a company that offered tuition reimbursement was that it allowed him to complete his education without the worries of unemployment. Sure, it may have taken him a little longer this way to complete his degree, but it got him out of warehousing. With a little creative problem solving, and some patience and persistence, there is always a way to work things out, even if it means taking a slower, backdoor route.

WHEN TO LEAVE YOUR JOB

If you are currently employed but are not able to pay your bills or adequately take care of your family, you may need to consider leaving your job for something better. First, discuss the situation with your boss. If you work for a small company and are told that they cannot afford to pay you any more money or that they cannot cover the cost of your health insurance, then it may be time to leave. If you have been promised raises or management training, but nothing has materialized over the last few years, then it is probably time to move on. However, if there *is* room to advance in your company but you do not have the qualifications or the proper educational level, then you know what to do next.

If you are currently employed in a job that pays an adequate salary but are bored, burned out, overly stressed, or generally unhappy with your job, the quickest way to improve your employment situation is to adjust your attitude. Experiment by adjusting your expectations or assigning less meaning to your job by developing a life outside of work. Try to avoid the vicious cycle of engaging in complaints or listening to negative talk at the lunch table. Recognize that some people thrive on complaining but never take any steps to improve their situation. Don't be one of them. Even if you feel the complaints are justified, or complaining makes you feel better in the short run, in the long run, complaining will only magnify the situation and waste everyone's time and energy without improving the situation. Realize that although you may not be able to control what goes on at the highest levels of your company, you can control what happens in your little corner of the company, at your work station, your desk, or in your office.

On the other hand, if you hate your boss and your job so much that you dread going to work in the morning or it's making you physically or emotionally ill, then you need to decide whether staying in your job is worth negatively affecting your health and peace of mind. If you no longer philosophically or ethically agree with your boss, or find yourself being left out of important meetings or discussions that impact your department, then that is probably a sign that you should move on. If your relationship with your boss or your coworkers is damaged beyond repair, or you are in a situation where you are not treated with respect and professionalism, then it's time to leave your job.

If you have done everything in your power to adjust your attitude or improve the relationship with your boss or coworkers and your situation still hasn't improved, then the next logical course of action is to change your location. Request a transfer to another department, or apply for a different position within your company, or search for a new job with a new employer. A friend of mine recently did just that. Although she enjoyed the company she worked for, she was so unhappy in her current position that she didn't think she could stand working there one more minute. So, when an opening came up in another department, she immediately applied for the position and got the job. Today, she is happier than she's ever been and enjoys a nice, quiet office with a wonderful boss and a new set of coworkers.

Any transition is going to feel funny or unsettling at first as you move away from the comfort of your old job. Change requires letting go of the old to reach forward and embrace the new. Be willing to tolerate a little anxiety and apprehension and consider it as a normal reaction to change. What a new career will bring is a fresh, new situation. Trust in yourself and the decision you've made. You are embarking on a new chance and a new beginning. Welcome to a new work world full of possibilities!

LEAVE ON GOOD TERMS

When you do leave a position, try to leave on good terms. First, inform your immediate supervisor and then tell your colleagues and department staff. Follow up any verbal resignation with a professionally written letter of resignation. Try to be gracious and frame your reasons for leaving in positive terms. Give at least two weeks notice (longer if you are in a management position) and offer to train your replacement. Finish up any projects you were working on and organize your files and notes so your successor can easily find them. Thank those who supported and mentored you along the way.

In general, it's probably wise to keep your plans for finding a new job to yourself until you have an actual job offer in hand. Once you tell your employer you are thinking about leaving, your relationship is never quite the same, and revealing your plans too soon may result in being replaced before you've found a new position. I once informed my boss two months in advance that I would be leaving my position to marry my husband and relocate to another state. Two weeks before I was to leave, I was laid off and subsequently lost two weeks of some badly needed salary.

Try to view your transition positively. Be aware that negative or bitter feelings may affect your ability to successfully interview for a new position. Employers are very cautious about hiring someone who does nothing but complain about their former job or employer. Whatever your reasons for leaving, leave your position as you arrived, on a professional basis. Remember, you want to create long-term career contacts. The old adage "Don't burn any bridges" is sound advice. You never know when you'll run across a former boss or coworker in the future.

IMPLEMENT YOUR DECISION

Whatever you have decided to do about your employment situation, now is the time to implement your action plan. Get things moving, create some momentum. If you stop now, you'll stagnate. By moving forward, you can guarantee you will not be in the same situation you were in two months or a year ago.

Monitor your progress and reward yourself for completing each step along the way. Make adjustments and changes when needed, but keep up the momentum. After planning out your steps, start with the first, complete it, and continue on to the next step until you achieve your goal.

Ultimately, you will want to move into a career that enables you to create the type of life you want. Although you probably wish this would happen more quickly and without so many strings, unfortunately, life has speed bumps along the way. There are many ways to move your career forward as well as your life. It will take persistence and dedication, but you have more control over your future than you realize through the choices you make and your attitude about those choices. The people I have worked with in the past who were able to find a better job or create a better future for themselves and their families did so because they were able to overcome their "yes, buts." If, after examining all of the options, you decide that it's impossible to leave your current job or go back to school, then at least make changes in your nonwork time to make your life more enjoyable. Then, begin to develop a long-term strategy to obtain a better job or a better living situation, even if this involves going back to school or switching jobs. Creating a better life takes planning, research, and sometimes time, but most of all courage! What is more important than improving the quality of your life or your family's life? Whatever the temporary hardship, keep the end result in sight because it's worth it!

CREATING BALANCE IN YOUR PROFESSIONAL AND PERSONAL LIFE

Strive to create balance among your work, social, home, and spiritual life. Burnout is a common problem in many careers, especially in positions that have a high level of people contact or stress and challenge. Burnout is a reaction to work stress that often leaves a person feeling drained and emotionally exhausted. Know your physical and emotional limits, when to establish boundaries, and how to maintain them. You will be of no help to anyone if you are so drained that you cannot function adequately. Take vacations, breaks, manage your time effectively, and learn how to diplomatically say "no" to prevent overload. There are only eight hours in a day and only so much work that can be accomplished in a given day. Although employers would like us to accomplish more in less time, with fewer resources, sometimes that is simply not possible. It is not weakness or ineptitude to ask for assistance when it is physically impossible for one person to complete a task that requires two or three people. Take care of yourself by getting enough rest, relaxation, exercise, and good nutrition to combat the effects of stress.

CAREER MANAGEMENT

Today, the trend is for employees to manage their own career trajectories rather than rely on the company to move them up the corporate ladder. Employees need to take charge of their own career destiny and make sure they are in a position to move up within the organization. In today's changing workplace, it is likely that the skills, knowledge, and abilities that allowed you to meet the requirements of your previous job will no longer correspond to the requirements of a future job. Benefits such as tuition reimbursement and in-house training programs have made it easier for employees to upgrade their skills.

From a job satisfaction perspective, you may get to a point where the old incentives and rewards provided by the organization no longer meet your current needs, values, and requirements. When this happens, a mismatch occurs between your values and the values of the company. From a career development or career management perspective, this is a sign that it's time to find a company that more closely matches your needs and values.

Career development assumes that a person's personal values and goals will change over his or her lifetime. Reexamining former career choices and establishing new goals and directions are all part of the career decision-making process. Although it might have once been enough to have a fast-track job with a great salary and all the fringe benefits, you may later desire to raise a family or pursue a hobby that has lain dormant since childhood. This is why we see so many high-profile career holders like lawyers, corporate executives, or financial brokers suddenly quit their jobs to become artists, nurses, or teachers. Or why some individuals suddenly decide to enter the priesthood or ministry late in life, often well after their families are grown or their spouses have passed away. This transition is not necessarily a mark of indecision or a sign of poor choices made in the past but an illustration of the way today's workers are responding to a changing world and a longer working life.

Career management goes beyond landing a first job and focuses on how to be successful in your overall career or in successive jobs over the course of your lifetime. Knowing what you need to do to be successful in your profession or move up in your organization is critical to career longevity. There are many simple commonsense things to being successful on the job and being able to keep that job:

- Coming to work on time
- Following company procedures
- Establishing good communication with your boss

- Getting along with your coworkers
- Being viewed as a dedicated or hard worker
- Not taking unethical advantage of your work situation and its resources
- Being cooperative and willing to do what's asked, maybe even volunteering for new assignments
- Being a team player, making a contribution
- Avoiding gossiping or engaging in behaviors that are irritating or offensive to others
- Performing a job well or maintaining quality in your work

These are the qualities that promotions are made from. Another key, but often overlooked, factor is being actively aware of how your performance is viewed by others, especially your boss. It's not a bad idea to occasionally ask for feedback about your performance at work, especially at the beginning of a new job, to avoid any surprises. Finding a mentor to help you negotiate work politics or to ask for advice in resolving or handling difficult situations is a strategy that has been successfully used by many career professionals.

Career experts state that the art of self-promotion, especially in a supervisory or management position, is one of the main reasons some people are promoted and others are not. Promote yourself by letting your boss know, at the appropriate time, when you have a good idea, finished an important project, or have run a successful campaign. Women have a tendency to underemphasize their accomplishments, thinking it makes them look like they're bragging to state their successes, whereas their male counterparts feel quite comfortable "tooting their own horn." Speaking up and calmly and factually describing a recent accomplishment is not bragging, it's just reporting what you or your department has been doing. And one final piece of advice: good managers always remember to acknowledge and give credit to those who helped them along the way.

Another component of career management is to review where you are in your career at least once a year and make any necessary changes or adjustments. In today's world, it may be wise to think about how you can recession-proof your job or, at the least, be able to land on your feet elsewhere if all else fails. One sure way is to add value at work by going above and beyond your basic job responsibilities. In the event positions are slated to be eliminated at your company, you may be seen as too valuable to be laid off. Likewise, if you had previously offered to become cross-trained, you may be able to quickly step into another position within your organization if your position is eliminated.

Here are some ways to recession-proof your job:

- Volunteer for extra assignments, volunteer to learn additional job responsibilities, or act as a backup for other positions in your department
- Keep a record of your accomplishments and any new skills you have acquired
- Make sure your boss is aware of your contributions and your value to the company
- Continue to upgrade your skills
- Keep your eyes open to new situations and opportunities that may arise

Keep current in your field by taking advantage of continuing education opportunities. In our ever-changing economy, education is one of the best ways to ensure marketability in your field. Many companies sponsor professional development opportunities, so take advantage of them. People in health care or technology careers especially need to remain current in their fields, or they quickly become obsolete.

As you develop self-confidence, skills, and experience, you will find it easier to broaden your range of options, thus enabling you to move into higher levels of responsibility or into job opportunities where you can make better use of your skills and abilities. None of your education or work experience is ever wasted. I still occasionally find myself using things I learned from my former (and now totally unrelated) undergraduate degree that I never thought I would use again.

Absorb and learn everything you can from your current job but know when to move on to a better opportunity when it presents itself. If you are self-employed, be ready to move your business to the next level when you can, but don't get too big, too fast, without the proper groundwork established. Use the decision-making tools you have learned throughout your career to identify new options and develop solid plans. In the future, you may decide to look for another position that offers even greater opportunities and salary potential. Or maybe you'll be able to propel a hobby into a full-time occupation. Most of us will continue to upgrade our careers in the form of better pay and advancement, less stress, better working conditions, less hours, and more job security.

The career management process doesn't stop once you get your first job, it continues throughout your lifetime. As you grow older and gain more experience, you will add to your achievements and develop new skills. You may even develop new interests and capitalize on new opportunities in new directions. Even after retirement, many of us will continue to work, grow, learn, and express ourselves creatively.

As the workplace continues to change, new jobs will appear and old ones will disappear. Technology will be the driving force behind many of these changes. Be aware of any trends or economic conditions that may affect your career or profession. As you adapt to each of these changes, recycle the skills you have learned by going through this process.

A friend of mine's husband was recently downsized when his company was sold to another firm. The entire IT staff was laid off, including all of the senior level programmers and network administrators. He applied for at least ten to fifteen positions, that I know of, for close to a year and reworked his resume multiple times. He would be invited in for an interview, would have a good experience, would think they liked him and his qualifications, but would not get the job. Sometimes it was because a position was eliminated as a result of internal company issues. Other times, he didn't know why he wasn't chosen, although he suspected that he was overqualified. He became very discouraged and even got a part-time job at an electronics store just to get out of the house and earn some extra cash. Five days before his unemployment benefits ran out, he was offered a position with a large financial services company.

What can we learn from this example? That perseverance is the key. If you are in the process of looking for a new job, try not to take rejections personally. People are rejected for lots of reasons, most having nothing to do with them personally. There is only so much you can do to get another person to hire you for a job, so learn what you can from the experience and just continue on to the next job interview. Like the football player who drops the ball, a certain amount of mental toughness is needed when searching for jobs. You must be able to shake off the disappointments and go on to the next play. Some may attribute finding a good job to luck, but luck won't occur if you just sit at home on the couch all day in front of the television. Opportunities are all around us. It's true that sometimes you have to be in the right place at the right time, but you certainly won't be around when opportunities surface if you aren't out there looking. Our IT candidate would never have known about the opening that led to his new job if he hadn't been actively searching for a job and hadn't made a personal inquiry at that particular company. As long as there are job openings to apply for and interviews to attend, there is hope. Job openings are like buses; another one will eventually come along.

Sample Resumes and Cover Letters

SAMPLE RESUME: CAREER CHANGE BECAUSE OF UNEMPLOYMENT

John Jones

123 Maple Drive	Phone: (570) 823-3456
Wilkes-Barre, PA 18702	E-mail: jjones@aol.com

Objective
Seeking to utilize 12 years of experience in the manufacturing industry to obtain a position maintaining and repairing Plumbing, Heating and Air Conditioning systems.

Profile
Over 15 years of experience in the manufacturing industry. First line supervisory experience in a union environment. Committed to quality control, team management.

Education
Luzerne County Community College
Nanticoke, Pennsylvania
Associate in Applied Science degree in **Plumbing, Heating and Air Conditioning**, 2008
United States Army, Fort Hood, TX
Certificate – Combat Telecommunication Operator

Certifications
ISO9000, ISO1400 Certification
EPA Refrigeration Certification

Work Experience
Techneglas, Pittston, Pennsylvania
Automated Technical Foreman   2000–2006
- Responsible for directing a unionized hourly shift workforce to maintain automated production equipment in a television glass finishing department.

- Directed set-up and maintenance personnel to maintain and repair automated production equipment.
- Diagnosed automated equipment breakdowns and processes.

Finishing Process Control Technician   **1994–2000**
- Performed shift process checks on finishing production equipment to maintain process parameters.
- Performed various surveys on incoming ware from forming department to determine finishing cycle times, stock removal, and finish quality.

Volunteer   Red Cross Blood Drive, 2004–present
Experience   Little League Coach, 2006–present

References   Available upon request.

SAMPLE RESUME: SINGLE PARENT REENTERING THE WORKFORCE

Barb Smith

123 Maple Drive	Phone: (570) 823-3456
Wilkes-Barre, PA 18702	E-mail: bsmith@aol.com

Qualifications Summary

Over 2 years Customer Service experience in a retail environment.
Proficiency with Microsoft Word and Excel. Demonstrated ability to successfully work with the public.
Good organizational skills and attention to detail.

Work Experience

Boscov's Department Store, Scranton, Pennsylvania   2 years
Sales Associate in Women's Fashion department.
St. Paul's Catholic Church and School, Scranton, Pennsylvania   5 years
Part-time church secretary. Answered the telephone, typed correspondence, scheduled appointments.

Volunteer Experience

Chair, annual church bazaar, St. Joseph's Church, 3 years.
Member, St. Joseph's Elementary School PTA, 2 years.

Education

Luzerne County Community College, Nanticoke, Pennsylvania
Associate in Applied Science degree in **Human Services**

References

Available upon request.

SAMPLE PLAIN TEXT RESUME SUITABLE
FOR JOB BOARD POSTING

JOHN JONES
1234 S. Apple Drive
Wilkes-Barre, PA
jjones@aol.com
570-823-9876

SUMMARY OF QUALIFICATIONS
* Executive Manager with over 10 years of management, purchasing, and sales experience in a high-volume manufacturing environment
* 10 years of experience managing a Fortune 500 manufacturing firm of over 100 employees
* Exceptional problem-solver with strong interpersonal and negotiating skills

SELECTED CAREER ACHIEVEMENTS
Management
* Successfully managed team of 50 sales professionals who increased sales profits

Sales and Marketing
* Launched successful promotional campaign for new product line

PROFESSIONAL EXPERIENCE
Executive Sales Manager, 2001–2006
ABC Manufacturing, Wilkes-Barre, PA
Senior Buyer, 1994–2001
Blue Steel Corporation, Scranton, PA

EDUCATION AND TRAINING
Bachelor of Science in Business Administration
University of Scranton, Scranton, PA

TECHNICAL SKILLS
Microsoft Office Suite, Peach Tree, Oracle

REFERENCES
Available upon request

SAMPLE COVER LETTER: INQUIRY

Jane E. Sample
3456 Westview Road
Milwaukee, Wisconsin 53226
(414) 771-2345

(Current Date)

Mary Peterson, Manager
Accounting Department
XYZ Company
10 Dear Park Drive
Chicago, Illinois 60622

Dear Ms. Peterson:

I am writing to introduce myself to you at the suggestion of Professor John Jones of Southern Milwaukee University. He has indicated to me that you are very interested in talking to senior Accounting students regarding possible career opportunities.

As you can see in the enclosed resume, I have a very strong academic background in Accounting combined with over five years' work experience in Accounting and Bookkeeping. My recent internship at American Insurance Company allowed me to develop and strengthen my technical and analytical/problem-solving skills through the successful completion of a major project involving the conversion of their accounting system. As Professor Jones indicated to me, because this type of conversion will be a major concern for your organization over the next year, I believe that I could make a significant and valuable contribution to that project, as well as in similar projects at your organization.

I would appreciate the opportunity to discuss how my education and experience is consistent with your needs. Please find enclosed my resume for your review. I will contact you early next week about the possibility of arranging an interview. Thank you for your time and consideration.

Sincerely,

Jane E. Sample

Enclosure

SAMPLE COVER LETTER: RESPONSE
TO AN ADVERTISED OPENING

Jane E. Sample
3456 Westview Road
Milwaukee, Wisconsin 53226

(Current Date)

Human Resources Department
Community Insurance Corporation
1212 West Center Road
Milwaukee, Wisconsin 53226

Dear Human Resources Manager:

I am writing to apply for the position of Customer Service Manager, as advertised in the April 28 issue of the *Milwaukee Journal*. With over five years' experience in customer service and a strong educational background in human resources management, I believe I could make a significant contribution in helping Community Insurance Corporation achieve its customer service goals and objectives.

As an example of my most recent accomplishments, I designed and implemented an incentive program that significantly increased productivity among customer service employees, which, in turn, significantly raised the level of customer satisfaction with the service provided. Because employee productivity and customer satisfaction are key components of a successful customer service operation, I believe that my expertise in these areas would be of particular value in meeting the challenges of this position.

The enclosed resume summarizes the full range of my skills and qualifications. I would appreciate the opportunity to discuss this position and my qualifications in more detail. Please feel free to contact me at (414) 771-2345 to arrange an interview. I look forward to hearing from you.

Sincerely,

Jane E. Sample

Enclosure

SAMPLE COVER LETTER: CAREER CHANGE
BECAUSE OF PLANT CLOSING

John Jones
123 Maple Drive
Wilkes-Barre, PA 18702

(Current Date)

Jim Davis, Manager
ABC Heating and Plumbing Corporation
1212 West Highland Boulevard
Wilkes-Barre, PA 18201

Dear Mr. Davis:

I am writing to apply for the HVAC position at ABC Heating and Plumbing Corporation as advertised in the *Sunday Times Leader*. I have over 12 years of industrial experience in a manufacturing setting. After my plant closed down, I had the opportunity to go back to school and earn an associate's degree in Plumbing, Heating and Air Conditioning, with an additional EPA certification in Refrigeration.

I have enclosed my resume for your review. I realize that I am making a career change, and am open to beginning my new career at a competitive, entry-level salary. I have a strong desire to return to the work that I enjoy and hope that you will consider my application favorably.

Please feel free to contact me at (570) 823-3456 to arrange an interview. Thank you for your consideration.

Sincerely,

John Jones

Enclosure

SAMPLE TELEPHONE CONVERSATION TO INQUIRE ABOUT POSSIBLE OPENINGS

"Good morning, Ms. Peterson, my name is Jane Sample. I am a senior accounting student in Professor John Jones's class. He suggested I contact you about possible career opportunities with your organization. Do you have a few minutes to speak with me? Thanks, I have a very strong academic background in Accounting plus an additional five years' work experience in accounting and bookkeeping. My recent internship at American Insurance Company allowed me to develop and strengthen my technical and analytical/problem-solving skills through the successful completion of a major project involving the conversion of their accounting system. Professor Jones indicated that this type of conversion will be a major concern for your organization over the next year. Is that correct?" (Allow time for Ms. Peterson to respond. Continue with the following as appropriate.) "I would appreciate the opportunity to get together with you at your earliest convenience to further discuss how my experience and credentials could fit with your company's needs. In the meantime, may I send you a copy of my resume?"

SAMPLE "COLD CALL" TELEPHONE CONVERSATION TO INQUIRE ABOUT POSSIBLE JOB OPENINGS

"Good Afternoon, Mr. Jones. My name is Jane Sample and I am calling to inquire about possible openings at your organization. I have over five years of accounting and bookkeeping experience and recently completed my associate's degree in Accounting at American University. Do you anticipate having any openings in the near future?" (Depending on how Mr. Jones responds, thank him for his time and offer to call him back in the future or send a copy of your resume, whichever is appropriate.)

SAMPLE THANK-YOU LETTER AFTER THE INTERVIEW

Jane E. Sample
3456 Westview Road
Milwaukee, Wisconsin 53226

(Current Date)

Ms. Terry Smith, Senior Manager
Community Insurance Corporation
1212 West Center Road
Milwaukee, Wisconsin 53226

Dear Ms. Smith:

I want to express my appreciation for the chance to visit with you regarding your opening for a Customer Service Manager at Community Insurance Corporation. I was impressed with your facilities and enjoyed meeting the staff.

I was particularly interested in our discussion of the customer surveys you are planning to develop over the next year. As we discussed, I recently completed a similar project where I designed a survey instrument that is now being used on a regular basis to measure customer satisfaction. The experience and expertise gained from this assignment would be especially beneficial in developing an effective tool to meet your needs.

Your position sounds like an exciting and challenging opportunity, and I want to reaffirm my strong interest in the position. I believe I can make a significant contribution to your customer service department. Thank you again for your time and I look forward to hearing from you.

Sincerely,

Jane E. Sample

Appendix B

Internet Resources

CAREER AND OCCUPATIONAL RESEARCH

- **America's Career InfoNet** (http://www.acinet.org). An excellent collection of career information including career videos.

- **Career Guide to Industries** (http://www.bls.gov/oco/cg). This guide provides detailed information on occupations by industry.

- **Guidance Resources Homepage** (http://www.wisemantech.com/guidance). Although originally designed for high school students, this is one of the most comprehensive collections of career and educational information for students of any age.

- **The Internet Public Library** (http://www.ipl.org/div/aon). A collection of over 2,000 Internet sites of professional and trade associations organized by occupational field.

- **Occupational Outlook Handbook** (http://bls.gov/oco). An excellent source of information about occupations from the U.S. Bureau of Labor Statistics.

- **O*NET** (http://online.onetcenter.org). A web-based resource for up-to-date descriptions and information on almost every career and occupation.

- **Princeton Review** (http://www.princetonreview.com/college/default.asp). Select "Majors Search" under "Careers" to learn about a variety of degrees and what colleges offer them.

- **Quintessential Careers** (http://www.quintcareers.com). A complete resource of career tips, information, and links to the best career and job related sources. Information and articles on career assessment and college planning. Special sections for high school students, college students, and job seekers.

- **State Occupational Projections** (http://www.projectionscentral.com). Select your state of interest for the expected employment growth for a particular occupation.

• **Vocational Information Center** (http://www.khake.com). A complete collection of links to everything you ever wanted to know about technical careers and technical education.

COLLEGES AND UNIVERSITIES

• **American Association of Community Colleges** (http://www.aacc.nche.edu). This site allows you to search for community colleges in the U.S.
• **College Board** (http://www.collegeboard.com). Select "Find a College" for informative articles about college and to use their college search engine.
• **List of Colleges and Universities** (http://www.utexas.edu/world/univ/alpha). An alphabetical list of U.S. colleges and universities with links to their homepages.
• **Peterson's Guide** (http://www.petersons.com). A comprehensive guide to all colleges and universities.

ENTREPRENEUR

• **Entrepreneur.com** (http://entrepreneur.com). A comprehensive collective of articles, advice, and resources for owning your own business.
• **My Own Business** (http://myownbusiness.org). A nonprofit organization dedicated to educating entrepreneurs by providing free coursework.
• **Small Business Administration** (http://www.sba.org). A collection of tools and resources for the small business owner.

FINANCIAL AID AND SCHOLARSHIPS

• **FAFSA** (http://www.fafsa.ed.gov). The official site of the Free Application for Federal Student Aid application form.
• **Fin Aid!** (http://www.finaid.org). An award-winning site that houses the most comprehensive source of student financial aid information, advice, and tools.
• **Scholarship Hunter** (http://www.scholarshiphunter.com). A free comprehensive scholarship and contest search site that does not require a student to submit personal information.
• **Student Aid on the Web** (http://studentaid.ed.gov). This is the Department of Education's free site, which contains information on funding your college education.

ISSUES FACING ADULT STUDENTS RETURNING TO SCHOOL

• **Back to College** (http://www.back2college.com). An informative site containing a variety of resources for adult students returning to school.

JOB SEARCH

- **CareerBuilder** (http://www.careerbuilder.com). This nationwide job board allows you to search for job openings, post your resume, and receive listings.
- **College Career Life Planning** (http://www.collegecareerlifeplanning.com). This noncommercial site provides access to more than 500 of the best free educational and career planning tools on the web for college students, career changers, and job seekers.
- **Federal Employment** (http://www.usajobs.opm.gov). The Federal Government employment information website.
- **Hot Jobs** (http://hotjobs.yahoo.com). This megasite allows you to search for a job or post your resume.
- **Job Hunter's Bible** (http://www.jobhuntersbible.com). This is the companion website to the book *What Color Is Your Parachute?* Contains tips and advice for job hunters.
- **Job Search USA** (http://www.jobsearchusa.org). Search for jobs anywhere in the U.S. by career or state.
- **JobWeb** (http://www.jobweb.org). Sponsored by the National Association of Colleges and Employers, this site lists jobs and provides information on career planning, resume and interviewing tips, employer profiles, and more.
- **Monster.Com** (http://www.monster.com). A monster-sized career site with something for job seekers at all stages of the job search.
- **The Riley Guide** (http://www.rileyguide.com). The Riley Guide offers advice on preparing for the job search process, resumes, researching employers, interviewing, and salary guides.

SALARY INFORMATION

- **America's Career InfoNet** (http://www.acinet.org). Find wage and employment trends for states and occupations as well as demographic and economic information.
- **Bureau of Labor Statistics** (http://www.bls.gov). This site provides a wealth of employment information. Select "Wages, Earnings, & Benefits" for salary information for various occupations in your area and elsewhere.
- **City Town Info** (http://www.citytowninfo.com/employment). An excellent source of unique facts about cities across the U.S. including job salaries.
- **Jobstar** (http://www.jobstar.org). Links and descriptions to over 300 salary surveys.
- **Salary.com** (http://www.salary.com). "Personal Tools & Resources" contains a searchable database for average salaries by occupation and state/metropolitan area.

SINGLE PARENTS

- **Parents Without Partners** (http://www.parentswithoutpartners.org). An international nonprofit organization that offers support, friendship, and the exchange of parenting techniques.
- **Single Parents Network** (http://www.singleparentsnetwork.com). A collection of single parent websites, articles, information, government resources, and online discussion forum support boards.
- **Single Parents Association** (http://www.singleparents.org). A membership organization for single parents formed to provide education, resources, friendship, and activities for single parents and their children.

STUDY SKILLS

- **Academic Success** (http://gwired.gwu.edu/counsel/asc). This site from George Washington University offers lessons to improve study habits and techniques.
- **Study Skills Self Help Information** (http://www.ucc.vt.edu/stdysk/stdyhlp. html). A great listing of tips and techniques for improving your study skills from Virginia Tech.

Notes

CHAPTER 1

1. Business and Professional Women's Foundation, "101 Facts on the Status of Working Women," Business and Professional Women's Foundation (2007), http://www.bpwusa.org/files/public/101FactsOct07.pdf (accessed January 8, 2008).

2. J. C. Franklin, "An Overview of BLS Projections to 2016," *Monthly Labor Review* 130, no. 11 (2007), http://www.bls.gov/opub/mlr/2007/11/art1full.pdf (accessed April 4, 2008).

3. J. J. L'Allier and K. Kenneth, "Preparing for Baby Boomer Retirement," *Chief Learning Officer* (2005), http://www.clomedia.com/contents/template/clo_article.asp?articleid=976&zoneid=25 (accessed June 11, 2008).

4. U.S. Census Bureau, (2004), "U.S. Interim Projections by Age, Sex, Race, and Hispanic Origin" (projected population of the United States, by age and sex: 2000 to 2050, Table 2a), http://www.census.gov/ipc/www/usinterimproj (accessed April 4, 2008).

5. A. S. W. Roper, "Baby Boomers Envision Retirement II, Key Findings: Survey of Baby Boomers' Expectations for Retirement," *AARP Bulletin* (May), no. 24 (2004), http://assets.aarp.org/rgcenter/econ/boomers_envision_1.pdf (accessed June 11, 2008).

6. S. Barr, "Pondering Alternatives to the Central Office," *Washington Post*, March 27, 2006, http://www.washingtonpost.com/wp-dyn/content/article/2006/03/26/AR2006032600807.html (accessed January 7, 2008).

7. Education Week, (2007), "More than 1.2 Million Students Will Not Graduate in 2007; Detailed Graduation Data Available for Every U.S. District and State," news release (June 12, 2007).

8. A. Dohm and L. Shniper, "Employment Outlook: Occupational Employment Projections to 2016," *Monthly Labor Review* 130, no. 11 (2007):86–125, http://www.bls.gov/opub/mlr/2007/11/art5full.pdf (accessed April 4, 2008).

9. Bureau of Labor Statistics, "Employment Projections: 2006–16," news release (December 4, 2007), http://www.bls.gov/news.release/ecopro.nr0.htm (accessed May 2, 2008).

10. Career Resource Network, "Job Skill Level Changes 1991–2005" (pie chart), North Dakota Department of Career and Technical Education, http://www.ndcrn.com/students/planning/Job_skill_level-charts.html (accessed April 11, 2008).

11. E. D. Pulakos, S. Arad, M. S. Donovan, and K. E. Plamondon, "Adaptability in the Workplace," *Journal of Applied Psychology* 85 (2000):612–24.

12. D. Desrochers, "Higher Education's Contribution to the Knowledge Economy," white paper. Solutions for our Future Project, http://tsp.convio.net/site/PageServer?pagename=resources_wp_desrochers_abstract (accessed April 4, 2008).

13. E. Chao, "Braving a New World," *AARP Bulletin* (September 2007), no. 32.

14. Ibid.

15. Bureau of Labor Statistics, "Employment Projections: 2006–16," news release (December 4, 2007), http://www.bls.gov/news.release/ecopro.nr0.htm (accessed May 2, 2008).

16. D. Sommers, "Getting Started," *Occupational Outlook Quarterly* (Fall), no. 2 (2007).

17. Business–Higher Education Forum, "An American Imperative: Transforming the Recruitment, Retention, and Renewal of Our Nation's Mathematics and Science Teaching Workforce," Business–Higher Education Forum (2007), http://www.bhef.com/news/AnAmericanImperative.pdf (accessed January 8, 2008).

18. Bureau of Labor Statistics, "Employment Projections: 2006–16," news release (December 4, 2007), http://www.bls.gov/news.release/ecopro.nr0.htm (accessed May 2, 2008).

19. The Information Company, "Job Hunting Tips for the Spring of 2008," *Careerism Newsletter* 38, no. 3 (2007):1–2.

CHAPTER 2

1. T. J. Terry, *Suddenly Single Mom: A Practical Guide to Self-Sufficient Survival* (Atlantic Beach, FL: T. J. Terry Publishers, 2006).

CHAPTER 3

1. J. B. Hurst and J. W. Shepard, "The Dynamics of Plant Closings: An Extended Emotional Roller Coaster Ride," *Journal of Counseling and Development* 64 (1986):401–5.

2. J. Stringham and D. R. Workman, *The Unemployment Survival Guide* (Salt Lake City, UT: Gibb Smith, 2004).

3. A. Siebert, *The Resiliency Advantage: How to Master Change, Thrive Under Pressure, and Bounce Back from Setbacks* (Portland, OR: Practical Psychology Press, 2005).

4. RSI-Therapy.com "RSI Statistics," http://www.RSI-Therapy.com (accessed April 4, 2008).

5. L. Hitchock, B. Ferrell, and M. McCaffery, "The Experience of Nonmalignant Pain," *Journal of Pain and Symptom Management* 9 (1994):312–18. For further reading, see W. W. Deardorff, "Depression and Chronic Back Pain. *Spine-Health.com* (October 15, 2004), http://www.spine-health.com/conditions/depression/depression-can-lead-chronic-back-pain (accessed May 30, 2008).

6. T. Grall, "Custodial Mothers and Fathers and Their Child Support: 2003 U.S. Census Bureau," (2006), http://www.census.gov/prod/2006pubs/p60-230.pdf (accessed April 11, 2008).

CHAPTER 5

1. R. J. Harvey, "Empirical Foundations for the Things-Data-People Taxonomy of Work," in *Things, Data, and People: Fifty Years of a Seminal Theory*, symposium presented at the Annual Conference of the Society for Industrial and Organizational Psychology, Chicago, April 2004, http://harvey.psyc.vt.edu/Documents/SIOP2004.Harvey.Fine.symposium.pdf (accessed May 30, 2008).

2. J. L. Swanson, and C. D'Achiardi, "Beyond Interests, Needs/Values, and Abilities: Assessing Other Important Career Constructs Over the Life Span, in *Career Development and Counseling: Putting Theory and Research to Work*, edited by S. D. Brown and R. W. Lent (Hoboken, NJ: John Wiley & Sons, 2005).

CHAPTER 6

1. F. Herzberg, B. Mausner, and B. B. Snyderman, *The Motivation to Work*, 2nd ed. (New York: John Wiley & Sons, 1959).

2. Salary.com, "Employee Job Satisfaction and Retention Survey 2007/2008: An Employer versus Employee Overview," PowerPoint presentation (2008). Salary.com, http://www.salary.com/docs/resources/JobSatSurvey_08.pdf (accessed June 20, 2008).

CHAPTER 7

1. M. Ghilani, "Reflections on a Theme of Buts," *Career Convergence* (April 2007), http://www.ncda.org (accessed April 2, 2007).

2. S. Choy, "Findings from the Condition of Education 2002: Nontraditional Undergraduates," National Center for Education Statistics NCES 2002–012, http://nces.ed.gov/pubsearch/pubsinfo.asp?pubid=2002012 (accessed January 8, 2008).

3. American Association of Community Colleges, "Community College Fast Facts," http://www2.aacc.nche.edu/research/index.htm (accessed April 6, 2008).

4. T. D. Synder, S. A. Dillow, and C. M. Hoffman, "Digest of Education Statistics: 2007," National Center for Education Statistics NCES 2008–022, http://nces.ed.gov/pubs2008/2008022.pdf (accessed April 8, 2008).

5. H. L. Holzer and R. L. Lerman, "America's Forgotten Middle-Skill Jobs: Education and Training Requirements in the Next Decade and Beyond," Washington, DC: The Workforce Alliance, no. 19 (2007), http://www.urban.org/UploadedPDF/411633_forgottenjobs.pdf (accessed April 4, 2008).

6. T. Zeiss, "Baby Boomers: An Encore Opportunity," *Community College Journal* 77 (2006):39–41.

7. K. A. Albert and D. A. Luzzo, "The Role of Perceived Barriers in Career Development: A Social Cognitive Perspective," *Journal of Counseling and Development* 77 (1999):431–36.

8. B. Weiner, "An Attributional Theory of Achievement Motivation and Emotion," *Psychological Review* 92, no. 4 (1985):548–73.

CHAPTER 9

1. R. E. Kutscher, "Historical Trends, 1950–92, and Current Uncertainties," *Monthly Labor Review* (November 1993):6–7, http://www.bls.gov/opub/mlr/1993/11/art1full.pdf; E. B. Figueroa and R. A. Woods, "Industry Output and Employment Projections to 2016," *Monthly Labor Review* (November 2007):54, http://www.bls.gov/opub/mlr/2007/11/art4full.pdf (accessed April 4, 2008). [For detailed employment information by industry].

2. Occupational Outlook Quarterly, "Education and Income: More Learning Is Key to Higher Earnings," *Occupational Outlook Quarterly* 50, no. 3 (2006):60.

3. American Association of Community Colleges, "Community College Fast Facts," http://www2.aacc.nche.edu/research/index.htm (accessed April 6, 2008).

4. U.S. Census Bureau, "Facts for Features, Women's History Month: March 2008," news release (January 2, 2008), http://www.census.gov/Press-Release/www/releases/archives/facts_for_features_special_editions/011179.html (accessed April 6, 2008).

5. W. J. Hussar and T. M. Bailey, "Projections of Education Statistics to 2016," The National Center for Education Statistics NCES 2008–060, no. 14, http://nces.ed.gov/pubsearch/pubsinfo.asp?pubid=2008060 (accessed April 8, 2008).

Index

About the Author

MARY E. GHILANI is a nationally certified counselor with 15 years of academic and career counseling experience with college students and adults. She is the Director of Career Services at Luzerne County Community College in Pennsylvania and the author of *Web-Based Career Counseling,* Her areas of expertise are career counseling, career assessment, and web-based resources. She is a member of the American Counseling Association, the National Career Development Association, and the National Association of Colleges and Employers. In addition to counseling younger students on career issues, she counsels older students as well as alumni and others in the broader community.